The Incest Diary

The Incest Diary

Farrar, Straus and Giroux   New York

Farrar, Straus and Giroux
18 West 18th Street, New York 10011

The study cited on page 19 is from the book *The Body Keeps the Score: Brain, Mind, and Body in the Healing of Trauma*, by Bessel van der Kolk, M.D. (New York: Penguin Books, 2014), page 31.

Library of Congress Cataloging-in-Publication Data
Title: The incest diary.
Description: First edition. | New York : Farrar, Straus and Giroux, 2017.
Identifiers: LCCN 2016041339 | ISBN 9780374175559 (hardback) | ISBN 9780374716493 (e-book)
Subjects: LCSH: Incest victims—Biography. | Sexually abused girls—Biography. | Sexually abused children—Biography. | Incest—Case studies. | Incest—Psychological aspects—Case studies. | Attachment behavior—Case studies. | Fathers and daughters—Case studies. | BISAC: BIOGRAPHY & AUTOBIOGRAPHY / Personal Memoirs. | FAMILY & RELATIONSHIPS / Abuse / Child Abuse.
Classification: LCC RC560.I53 I52 2017 | DDC 618.92/858360092 [B]—dc23
LC record available at https://lccn.loc.gov/2016041339

Designed by Abby Kagan

Our books may be purchased in bulk for promotional, educational, or business use. Please contact your local bookseller or the Macmillan Corporate and Premium Sales Department at 1-800-221-7945, extension 5442, or by e-mail at MacmillanSpecialMarkets@macmillan.com.

www.fsgbooks.com
www.twitter.com/fsgbooks • www.facebook.com/fsgbooks

1 3 5 7 9 10 8 6 4 2

Author's Note

I believe everyone has the right to tell her or his story. For many reasons, in telling mine, I have chosen to be anonymous. I have changed many specifics in order to preserve my anonymity. But I have not altered the essentials. I ask the reader to respect my wish to remain anonymous.

The Incest Diary

One of the therapists I lied to was a beautiful woman whose father had studied with Freud. I liked her until we got closer to the incest. When I was in college, I went to see her on Thursday afternoons. We circled around my family and I lied about my relationship with my father. One day she told me that she was concerned about me being at risk for self-harm. She wanted me to see a psychiatrist she worked with who would give me medication. I walked out of her office and never saw her again. She left me several voice mails over the following weeks wanting to know if I was all right. I never called her back.

In the fairy tales about father-daughter incest—"The Girl Without Hands," "Thousand Furs," the original "Cinderella," "Donkey Skin," and the stories of Saint Dymphna, patron saint of incest survivors—the daughters are all as you would expect them to be: horrified by their fathers' sexual advances. They do everything in their power to escape. But I didn't. A child can't escape. And later, when I could, it was too late. My father controlled my mind, my body, my desire. I wanted him. I went home. I went back for more.

The last time I had sex with my father was at the beach house on the island when I was twenty-one. I spent a week there with my father and my brother, who had just turned nineteen. The three of us hadn't spent a week together in many years; I hadn't spent much time with my father since I left home at seventeen. I hadn't been to the family beach house for several years. The gray shingled house with many porches and white shutters next to the water. With the American flag on the old pole near the white front gate.

That week with my father and brother, I wore a blue bikini top. The bottoms were bright red. My father wanted me. I felt his eyes on my shoulders and neck, on my legs, my breasts, and my hips. I held my body differently when I knew he was looking. I wanted to be sexy. I walked differently when I knew he was watching me from behind. Watching me as I walked back and forth from the house to the shore. Watching me take off the white shirt

I wore over my bathing suit when I sat to read before I swam. I wanted him, too. I wasn't a child anymore. I wasn't even a teenager. I was a grown-up. My body was a woman's body.

We played bridge with some of the neighbors in the house just up the road. They told me stories about myself as a little girl playing on the beach—how much I loved the big waves—and stories about my grandparents, around the time when they bought the house in the 1960s. We played pinochle with my brother. We drank gin and tonics on the east porch.

I spent my childhood summers in that house, and as a little girl I slept in that same upstairs bedroom. Many of my few happy childhood memories are from that place.

The first two nights I couldn't stop masturbating, thinking about my father being so close. At the other end of the house, alone, sleeping in the bed with the walnut headboard. I couldn't help it. I wanted and I didn't want him to come in and fuck me. On the third night he did.

I remember my father opening the old, heavy door to my bedroom. I wanted my father to open the door. I wanted him to come in. I wanted to hear him come in to the bedroom with the yellow-and-blue bedspread and

5

the bookcases built into the walls holding my grandfather's complete Sir Walter Scott. Into the room with the curtains patterned with red sailboats on white fabric and the bird's-eye-maple-framed mirror and the closet with yellow raincoats and army-green galoshes and the large wool flannel shirts hanging on wooden hangers inside. The closet with a plaid umbrella and spare flip-flops.

My father pulled off the bedspread and saw my twenty-one-year-old body. I was naked and I was wet. I wanted his big hard cock deep inside me. I was very wet. I wanted him inside me all the way up. I had never felt sexier. My body was pure sex. My father had made himself a sexual object for me, too. I objectified him as I objectified myself for him. I had an orgasm bigger than any single one I had in my subsequent twelve-year marriage. We didn't say anything. Not one word. Then he got out of my bed, went out of the room and down the hall and back into his bed. Not one word ever about that night.

He fucked me and he made me come. We never kissed. We didn't kiss that night, and we didn't kiss when I was a teenager, and we didn't kiss when I was eleven or ten or nine or eight or seven or six or five or four or three.

He never put his tongue inside my mouth.

That week on the island, I told Katherine Huntington, a family friend and neighbor, the truth about my father having sex with me. I told her what happened when I was a young child. I did not dare tell her about the night that had just passed—but I did confide in her about my childhood. I wasn't the only one who thought she was a remarkable woman. She was the opposite of my mother—she was extraordinarily capable, warm, independent. People adored her. I looked up to her and wanted to grow up to be like her. When I was little, she made me feel special. She would ask my opinion on things and squat down to listen to me. When I was a teenager, she told me that I was clever and courageous.

I always thought she was beautiful, strong, and brave. She loved to sail by herself. She could read, write, and speak Mandarin. She and her second husband spent a year driving across Africa. She was a volunteer firefighter in the little beach community. The only time she didn't wear heels was when she drove the fire truck. She would cook dinner by herself for dozens of people and her house was always full of guests. She had a greenhouse behind the main house where she grew gardenias and plumerias. Once, she found a baby bobcat by her greenhouse door. She gave it a bowl of milk and hoped it would reunite with its mother. But another neighbor told her that he had seen a dead bobcat in the road down by the market. Katherine took in the baby bobcat and gave it all the maternal love she had given her children. She gave it lamb for supper, with a dish of whipped cream afterward.

My grandparents had been close friends of her parents. I was close to two of her children and a niece and a nephew. I felt happy being around her family. I wished she would take *me* in.

The week that I was at the beach with my father and brother, Katherine and her husband asked me over for dinner. I asked Katherine if we could speak in private. She said of course, and took me upstairs to her bedroom. We sat on her enormous white bed with its dozens of soft linen-cased pillows. I held one of the pillows close to my chest while I told her that my father had raped me when I was a little girl. I told her that I felt like I was going crazy and I didn't know what to do. She leaned over to me and I thought she was going to embrace me, but she put her hand over my mouth. "Get over it," she said. "Don't talk about it. Forget it, and get over it." She then told me that she had been molested when she was a child. She said her parents knew and didn't do anything about it. "But these are things to forget and get over," she said. She told me to go home to my father and not to talk about it anymore. She was never the same with me again. She wasn't friendly anymore and she avoided me the rest of that trip.

One afternoon, a year or so after that week on the island, I confronted my father about our incestuous relationship. He and my brother had been playing tennis. We left my brother and went for a walk in the suburban neighborhood where my father lived. My father told me that I had seduced him when I was a little girl. I reminded him that I was just a toddler when it began. He replied that I was such a smart, precocious child, so curious about everything, and I wanted him to touch me; I had asked him to feel how soft it was. He was so lonely in those days because my mother was sick, in the worst of her depression, and he said that she was cold and cruel to him. All she was interested in was steeplechasing and horses; she never asked him questions about his life, his interests. She belittled him—the job he had, the clothes he wore. She wanted more money, she wanted him to make her happy, and he was working so hard and never made enough money. He told me that, during those years, he was so tired and I was his shining light of joy. He said he was sorry. He clenched his jaw and opened his eyes wide while he looked down at the pavement where we walked and repeated that he was sorry.

A day after that conversation, he told me again that he was sorry for all he'd done. He cried and said he was sorry for getting what he needed from my mother from me instead. A day after that, he called and asked me to come and talk to him. He said that if I was going to persist in my allegations about him having raped me, then I was no longer his daughter. He told me that I was dead to him. I can only assume that he'd spoken with a lawyer, and that this is why he started using the word *allegations*, and why he no longer admitted to our incest, but denied it. He told our family about my *allegations*. My grandfather tried to have me committed to a mental hospital, but there were no grounds. My aunt called me in the early hours of my birthday morning to tell me that she was on my father's side. That was when my brother dropped out of college. My brother had always played violin, he was a serious violinist, but he stopped playing. He locked himself in his bedroom for days at a time. He cried and said that he didn't know whom to believe. One night he told me that he had considered suicide because of what had happened to our family.

My father told his friends, too. One of my father's friends called and asked me to coffee. He told me that he was there for me, that he understood my pain. He cried and told me about being molested when he was a boy. We went from drinking coffee to drinking wine. He told me about his pain, his silence, how it fucked him up.

A month after I confronted him, my father quit his job and he traveled. I didn't hear from him for months, until he sent me a card from Australia. On the front of the card was a baby rabbit in a field of wildflowers. Inside he'd written: *Get well soon.*

I felt completely responsible for my brother's breakdown. I couldn't stand it; from week to week he seemed more depressed and anxious. I was afraid he would kill himself. So I told him not to worry, that it didn't happen. I told him it must have been someone else who raped me. My brother started to get better. He and I have never spoken about it since.

When our father came back, I took him out to dinner at a place I liked and we ate a beet and arugula salad for an appetizer. I told my father that someone else must have raped me, and from then on I wasn't going to talk about the past. I told him that it didn't matter anymore. My father didn't say anything. Then he asked me if I would like to go see a movie in a couple of weeks. I said sure, even though I didn't want to, but I felt relieved that the family was getting back to normal.

The world is full of work to do
A little rest and then
The world is full of work to do
Sing hushabye loo, low loo, low lan
Hushabye loo, low loo

This is the song my mother sang me to sleep. Then later my father would come into my room. Sometimes he would penetrate me, sometimes he would masturbate onto my body. He said he couldn't help it. He told me it was my fault. It must have been my fault. He said that he couldn't help it because I was so beautiful and it felt so good. He said he was a sick man. A weak victim of his desire. And I, too, felt desire; I felt my wildness. Sometimes I rubbed myself on his hairy thigh. I did it because it felt good.

———

Strawberry was my father's favorite kind of jam. One morning when I was five or six, he put strawberry jam on his penis and asked me to lick it off. I remember the sweet and the slime of the fruit combining with the sweet and the slime of the man.

I abused my dolls. Ken didn't have a penis, so my Barbie got fucked by my brother's dinosaurs. The horns of the pentaceratops went up and down hard on her plastic crotch. I cut off her hair. I dyed it green and red with food coloring. I beheaded her by pulling off her head. I hated her. She embarrassed me; she was disgusting.

I had a book about how babies are made. There were anatomical drawings of a man and a woman. I remember wondering why they didn't also have a drawing of a little girl when they explained how the penis goes into the vagina.

Sometimes fucking me made my father very happy. And sometimes it made him very angry. When I remember the day in the bathtub, I can only see it either from above, watching the two of us, or from my father's perspective. I see the terrified girl. She's moving in the bathwater to get away from him. But there is nowhere to go. The tub is so slippery it is hard to move, and the water sloshes about when she does. He is furious and he is lunging down at her while she cries and sloshes around in the bathwater. The water is full of blood. She is in a bath of blood. Her own blood. He did it again to her, went up into her too far, fucked her too hard and made her bleed. It made him angry. *I will kill you if you tell anyone. I will kill you I will kill you I will kill you.*

My mother had art books in the bookcase in the living room. I spent a lot of time looking through them. In Jacques-Louis David's *The Death of Marat*, Marat was killed in the bath. I was almost killed in the bath but I wasn't. I could look at his murdered body in the bath and still be alive.

For my eighteenth birthday, my mother sent me nine drawings in a manila envelope. They were copies of self-portraits she had done when she was pregnant with me—one for each month. Included with the drawings was a copy of a journal entry from my father dated two days after I was born. The copy was on pink paper and the entry was three paragraphs long. He wrote about the cold, the spring, the way the moon hung the night I was born. My father wrote about being so happy to have a child. The entry ends, *Some day this kid's gonna fuck.*

My father wanted to fuck me, and sometimes he wanted to kill me. Sometimes it was both. I don't know how many times he cut me with a knife. Sometimes he was threatening to kill me with it, other times he cut inside my pussy. Was he trying to circumcise me? Maybe he was trying to cut my pleasure out, to remove his pleasure.

When I was two and a half years old, my brother was born. It was a complicated birth. My mother was never quite the same after, my father said. She also suffered what might have been postpartum depression, but was never diagnosed. She stopped producing milk after only a few months of breastfeeding my baby brother, probably because she barely ate. She preferred to be alone, or, when she felt well enough, with her horses. We didn't make her happy. She cried a lot, and her sadness was bottomless. Sometimes she was vicious to us, sometimes she was sweet. I only remember her happy around her horses or when preparing for Christmas.

My father looked at me with hunger. He looked at my mother with disdain. He thought I was born for him.

And I thought my brother was born for me. Who did my mother belong to and who was born for her? No one. Except her horses. She laughed once telling a friend that she dreamed of horses almost every night, but never dreamed about us. The love of her life was steeplechasing. She boarded her horses, Hookah and Stradivarius—one a beautiful buckskin and the other a chestnut—at her friend's small horse farm.

I can see the image of my father with the knife over my head, and I don't feel frightened. Numb, but not scared. But when I remember the sounds—his footsteps coming up the hall leading to my room, the sound of the door opening, his breathing, the sheering sound of the metal blade being pulled from the sheath—then I freeze and go outside my body. It was a buck knife, the same one he used on camping trips. He used it to sharpen a willow branch to pierce marshmallows and roast them. He used it to sever cord for tying the tent down in a windstorm. My father pulled the knife out and had that dead, cold look in his eyes and his jaw was clenched. But then he realized that I was awake, watching him holding the knife over me. He turned away, the knife shaking in his hand, and he left my room holding the sheath in one hand and the shaking knife in the other. The other day I read a story about a woman who killed her two young daughters while they slept. She doesn't remember doing it. Now she wants to know if her daughters are all right. I wonder about my father. Would he remember if he had cut me up with the buck knife? Maybe not. Maybe he would have wondered afterward if I was all right.

My mother didn't like camping. She hated being at the cabin in Maine. I remember my father making dinner on the woodstove. She didn't like dinner cooked on a woodstove. She didn't like being away from her horses. My father loved using kerosene lamps when it got dark, and my mother hated them and missed a house full of electric lights. She was afraid, too, that we would forget to blow one of the lamps out and that the cabin would burn down.

My father went to gather wood for the fire. Then he got down on his knees and laid the fire in the belly of the big cast-iron stove. He lit it with a match he struck on the side of the stove. I liked to watch the newspaper catch the flame and get devoured. He blew on the fire. He shut the stove door as it began to rage. I listened to the low roar of the fire. He put on a pot of water to boil.

In the cabin were beautiful colored-glass cups. They shone like jewels. Deep, rich colors. Teal, turquoise, golden ocher, royal blue, purple, scarlet, fuchsia, silver gray. I loved drinking water out of those colored cups with question-mark-shaped handles. They were kept in the same wooden hutch as a drawer that held spices in little jars sealed with shaved-down corks. I liked to open that drawer, pull out the tiny corks, and smell the spices.

I remember the red-stripe ticking on the mattress in the bed where I slept. My father took off my pants and my underwear. I remember being facedown, biting the button on the mattress while my father put something inside me. I felt him rub his penis between my butt cheeks. I ran my tongue along the button I was biting. I remember the taste of the mattress. Smoky canvas. The smell of the mattress. Old fabric, firewood smoke, musty smell.

A mouse who lives in a warm nest where it is well fed will venture out and then, when frightened, rapidly return to its home. A mouse who has an uncomfortable nest—where it experiences pain and lack of food—when out of its nest in a place with warmth and food, and then suddenly frightened, will *also* return home, just like the other mouse. Experiments with other animals proved the same—when an animal is scared, it goes home, no matter how terrifying home is.

I climbed on a stool and opened the medicine cabinet over the bathroom sink and took out a bottle of my mother's Nivea lotion. I unscrewed the top and left it inside the cabinet. I liked the smell because it was the smell of my mother. I sought comfort from her in her scent since I didn't have it from her directly. I carried around the lotion bottle and smelled it while I sucked my thumb. Smell and suck, smell and suck. Smell the sweet perfume, suck my soothing thumb. I made my thumb turn white and withered with all the sucking. I sucked it all the time until my dentist, who called me Princess, told me I would get buck teeth if I kept it up. He told me he would be proud of me for quitting, and I wanted my dentist to be proud of me. But I like to have things in my mouth.

When I was very little, I couldn't sleep because of my nightmares and I peed in my bed every night. A few times at the grocery market, I walked up to a stranger who looked nice and asked if they would take me home with them. I was difficult at my school. I hit the boys. I drew coiled cobras in beds and girls being impaled by large buildings. When we went on a family trip to Boston and New York, I had strong pains in my body, because every time I looked at the big tall buildings I felt that they were about to fuck me. I wondered if I was pregnant all through first, second, and third grades. I obsessively masturbated. I had open sores on my hands from washing them over and over until they bled.

But to my mother, I was the other woman. She often told me that she wished I hadn't been born.

For discipline, my father tied me to a chair. Sometimes he put the chair in the closet. Over time, I learned not to scream. I learned that eventually my father would come and let me out.

I remember looking at a painting in a book of a woman wearing a white dress hanging off of a bed. An evil, ugly monster was sitting on her belly. It scared me and excited me to look at her. It also excited me to look at the painting, in my mother's book of the Louvre, of the two women, topless, where one is pinching the other's nipple. I looked at the saints with eyes plucked out, bodies pierced by arrows, Saint Bartholomew skinned. I looked at the pictures of the Sabines being abducted. And Judith slaying Holofernes. I looked and looked and ran my finger over that bleeding, murdered man.

Years later, when I saw Botero's paintings of prisoners at Abu Ghraib, blindfolded and restrained, it excited me.

Botero paints all the prisoners as very fat. They are easier to look at fat. I like to be gagged and restrained. It makes me think of the time my father tied me up in the closet and face-fucked me until he came in my mouth and I vomited up the semen. I'm thinking of me as a very fat five-year-old girl and my father as a fat Botero man, naked but for his hat.

My mother blamed me for everything that wasn't right in our house. She even blamed me for my father's hair going completely white before he was thirty years old. She called me *whore*, *bitch*, *fucking bitch*, and *little shit*. My least favorite was being called *little shit*. Maybe I was a whore and a bitch and a fucking bitch. But I wasn't a little shit.

I remember my mother telling me many times that life is about two things—sex and the fear of death.

My father is my secret. That he raped me is my secret. But the secret under the secret is that sometimes I liked it. Sometimes I wanted it, and sometimes I seduced him and made him fuck me. I have seen therapists and psychiatrists and psychologists and analysts, and I told them about missing my grandparents. I talked about missing my three friends who died. I talked about my mother slapping me hard across the face and then crumpling into a pile on the floor, weeping, telling me she was terrible, such a terrible mother. And I would comfort her and tell her not to worry, it didn't hurt very much and I was fine. I did tell a few of them that my father molested me. And if they wanted to talk further about it, I stopped the conversation. I never told any of them the whole truth about me and my father.

Today I read in a book about torture that the more a captive is raped, the more likely she is to experience pleasure. Pleasure as a means of survival. The more she is raped. The more pleasure. Does this mean I have felt the most pleasure in the world? My body is pure rapture. Writing this arouses me. I think about my father and I get wet. I think about my father and I feel him in my pussy.

Pleasure as a means to survive. My father is my sexual pleasure. I'm tied up and he's hand-feeding me his semen. Hand-feeding me what he just jacked off into his palm. This great pleasure of ours is bursting in light. I feel God in my heart getting bigger. I'm swallowing his sperm while I'm bound to the chair, and I have rays of light shooting out of my head and face.

———

I get warm, soft buzzing feelings when I think about that. Being locked in the closet tied up, waiting for him, waiting for my father to rescue me after he hurt me. He rescued me. I was so relieved. So happy when the closet door opened and he untied me, undoing the knots holding me to the chair. He let me out, he let me run. I ran out into the sunshine.

How could I not love the man who set me free?

was afraid of fire. I was afraid of the house burning down. Afraid of my body being burned. But I burned my body. I burned my own body. I needed to feel pain. I remember that gray gas heater.

My mother got me out of the bath, I was very young. She told me to dry myself off while she went into the other room. I sat down on the heater. I remember the burning smell of my skin. I remember the silver metal table at the emergency room. The doctors in blue gowns and white face masks. They cut off my pants. I remember the gooey ointment and the sound of medical tape being torn and the feel of it sticking to my bottom to hold the bandages in place. A nurse told me that I had second-degree burns. She explained to me that burns are the opposite of murder. Third-degree burns are the worst, but third-degree murder is the least severe. She also told me a joke that I then repeated to everyone I met. What is brown and sticky?

A stick.

Claude Lévi-Strauss wrote that the key difference between animals and humans is incest prohibition. What does this make me?

I remember one time in my bed watching my father's enormous penis riding my flat-breasted chest—the fleshy head coming at me, erupting in fluid that got everywhere, but I especially remember it pooling in my belly button.

My mother was terrified that if I played outside barefoot I would cut myself and get tetanus. She was afraid, too, when I had a paper cut that it would get infected and kill me like that lady in Alabama. But when I showed her the blood between my legs when I was very small and, on a different day, blood on my unicorn-patterned sheets, she said nothing, she did nothing.

I wanted to hurt myself when I cut my thigh with a paring knife. One morning while my mother was making coffee, I sliced my leg with a knife. She told me not to get the blood on the carpet where I sat. It felt good to have that kind of pain, a different kind of pain, but I remember the shame I felt when she didn't care.

My school was concerned about my abdominal pains, and, once, I was rushed to the hospital to have an emergency appendectomy. But it was because I hadn't shit for a month.

When my second-grade teacher told us the story of Scheherazade, I felt I was like her. Every night she had to save her life. Every night I had to save mine, too. My father told me that he would kill me and himself if he couldn't have me.

When I was five or six, I realized that having a sibling meant that my parents had had sex. I knew how babies were made and I was furious. I didn't like my father having sex with both of us. A man sleeping with his wife and her daughter, his daughter.

I know people with better memories than mine, but mine is better than most. I think part of it is just that I have a good memory and part of it is something I don't understand. But I don't have a good memory about everything. I have large gaps and blurs. There was one house my family lived in for more than a year, and I have only one memory of my father in that house—and it's of him fucking my mother. She was in her nightgown, and he was on top of her, humping, naked, one leg bent up toward his chest. When my mother and I

27

had the one conversation that we ever had about sex, which happened when I was seventeen years old—just before I left home—she told me that she loved having sex with my father, and that was what she missed most about him. She told me that he used to have sex with her while she was sleeping.

Some memories didn't come to me until I was older. Many things I have forgotten and might never remember. The feelings are stuck in my body and my body remembers everything. But many of my memories are fractured, shattered, pieces here and there. A smell, a sound. A burst of fear. Sometimes they make me feel frozen and paralyzed and I forget who and where I am. The smell of diesel fuel. The smell of strawberries. The scent of dried sage. The feel and smell of blood and slimy semen between my legs. Sometimes now, after I have sex during my period, I don't wash immediately afterward, but I lie in bed and I look and I see and feel and smell where and how I was hurt. Some things that still make me freeze and feel terrified are the sounds of moaning and of a door being carefully closed. The rustling sounds of clothes being carefully removed and dropping to the floor.

My memory is better than my brother's, but he remembers some things that I don't. And my mother remembers some things that we don't. But she refuses to remember our unhappiness.

Does my father remember what it feels like to have his penis inside a three-year-old girl? He says that the years when I was little were the happiest years of his life.

On the nights when my father didn't do anything to me, I felt abandoned. I loved him. Sometimes it was weeks, sometimes months, maybe a year, I don't know how long, but sometimes he didn't fuck me and he didn't masturbate over my bed while I was supposed to be sleeping. Why was he leaving me alone? Why was he neglecting me? Did he not love me as much anymore? Was I not good enough anymore?

When my brother began to walk and run, it was summer. I remember him running naked and I looked at his little penis. I was excited that I now had a little body to play with—and a body with a little penis. But then, when I was holding his little body, I decided that I would take care of him instead. I slipped up one day, though, while we sat naked in the sandbox. I asked him if he "wanted to fuck." He still didn't talk and could not answer me. But after I explained how the man inserts his penis into the woman's vagina, an enormous wave of guilt washed over me, and I was filled with shame, and I jumped out of the sandbox. I never said anything to him about it again. I started praying to God that I hadn't harmed him. It became my nightly prayer. For years, until I was a teenager, I told God that I would do anything if He would please help my brother not be harmed by what I did.

My father still excites me and he still scares me. When I think about him, I feel aroused. I feel tightness, constant awareness, and sometimes very sharp pains in my pussy. My gut is tight and it feels dark. My throat feels constricted, like I can't breathe. My pulse quickens. My hands shake. I fall into a trance, as if I'm in another world and not in control of myself at all. I feel like throwing up. I would do anything he tells me to do. I want to please him and also to murder him. I need to be obedient to him and to make him laugh and smile and feel pleasure. I want him to be proud of me. I want him to think that I'm clever. I want him to think that I'm sexy. And I want to savagely mutilate his body and feed his corpse to dogs.

was maybe eight years old, and I told my mother that I loved her. She said that I told her that too much. *You don't need to tell me every day.* So I stopped telling her that I loved her.

I don't look in her eyes. I look at the bridge of her nose when I speak with her. I look at myself reflected in her glasses. I watch her hands, her nervous fingers twiddling about. Always moving. She can't sit still.

I remember a friend of mine coming over for dinner at my mother's house a couple of years after my parents had separated—I was twelve or thirteen. I was cooking dinner for my mother and brother and my friend Francine. As I cut up vegetables for a salad, Francine said to me, "I can't believe how many mean things your mother says to you. So much mean teasing." I hadn't noticed. Sometimes she was so sweet to me, and proud of me. But she slapped me, backhanded my face, called me names, falsely accused me of lying, smoking. "You hate the people you love the most" was something she liked to tell my brother and me.

One time I remember her walking into my room, where I was quietly playing with my dollhouse, and screaming at me that she hated me.

She still wants me to ride horses with her. She wants me to steeplechase, too. But I don't give a fuck about steeplechasing. I hug her rarely, but when I do, I try not to breathe in her smell of sandalwood and cat.

My mother taught me to be afraid to talk about money. My mother told me to be very, very careful of how much I eat so that I don't get fat. She taught me to be afraid of butter, afraid of walking on street grates, afraid of strange dogs, afraid of germs on public door handles, afraid of the sun. She taught me to hate the people I love the most.

I feel compelled to tell my mother gory things. I tell her things I read about in the news or in history books. I tell her details about the bloodshed in Sierra Leone and about the massacres of Badr Khan. I can't help it. All I want to do is to tell her stories of violence. It comes from a deep rage that I can't express to her. A desperate need for her to face the truth, which she refuses to acknowledge and probably never will. More than everything my father did to me, it hurts me that she denies it. I show her pictures of the slain beauties at La Specola, the natural history museum in Florence. The eighteenth-century figures of pretty murdered women with their innards exposed—intestines and livers and stomachs, hearts, kidneys spilling out of their perfectly made, peeled-open, and glowing wax skin. Their faces are peaceful; they wear pearls; they lie on beds of lace.

I also like telling her about beautiful things coming out of terrible things. Like the beetles who can lay their eggs only in the charred trees left by a forest fire. New life in the wake of destruction. I also feel the need to remind her of triumph. It comes from a fierce rage, too.

My brother lives in Charleston now. He and his wife are both surgeons. They have three daughters and two hypoallergenic dogs. My brother and I would both say that we are close. We trade recipes, we talk about cooking and food, his daughters. But we don't talk about the rest of it. There is a closeness, though. It's as if we are very, very close—too close, even—in one way and galaxies apart in every other way. We are close because of everything we don't—and probably never will—talk about. He doesn't know that us both having heard the sounds of our father masturbating in the other room, in the bed with the French doors open to the light rain, makes us closer, but it does. Closer and farther away at the same time.

We don't talk about the times our father screamed at me and choked me while my little brother watched. My brother and I don't talk about the one time we did talk about all that happened. My brother needed it to be untrue. He still needs all of it to be untrue.

t makes my palms sweat remembering how my father asked me if I wanted to fuck when I was little. He asked me in baby talk if I wanted to fuck. Yes, I replied, let's fuck.

I wasn't afraid of my father. My father was the one who fed me, got me dressed, took me to school, made me pasta, bathed me, dried me off with a towel, brushed my teeth. Thoughts of monsters were what kept me from falling asleep—hidden under my sheets, trying not to move or breathe.

There were two fathers, so there must have been two of me.

I masturbated with the smooth back of my little wooden hairbrush. I felt ashamed, but it felt so good. I would be overcome with desire, and I would feel the desire here, in my pussy, and I would rub the back of the hairbrush along my pussy. Secretly, quietly. Full of shame and remorse. Hoping I wouldn't need to do it again. But I would. When I was a little older, sometimes I thought about a boy named Harry while I rubbed myself. I remember the wood of the hairbrush covered in my slimy wet.

I was too shy to stick out my tongue around other people. Would they be able to tell that this tongue had licked a penis? Would my tongue give me away? My vagina looked like a bird. Like how you draw a bird—an *m* in the sky, with soft tips, like a McDonald's *m*. When I looked down at my vagina, the pudgy lips were like a fleshy bird. This made me uncomfortable when I drew birds, because then maybe everyone else would know what I looked like naked. Would they be able to tell that my vagina looked like a bird? And if they knew my pussy looked like a bird would they know that my father rubbed his penis on it and that he fucked me? And would they know then that it was my fault?

I tried to run away once. I packed a green houndstooth suitcase full of Cheerios and pennies. I made it to the far road. I sat down on a rock and opened the suitcase. I ate the Cheerios. I sat in the sun. I looked around at the bushes and the trees and I looked up at the sky and the clouds. I got thirsty; I went home.

People told me I was a pretty girl. I remember thinking about pretty, and thinking about sexy. I remember the feeling of being desired. Sometimes it was like a power I had. And sometimes it was more frightening than a power.

I got a new black-and-white bathing suit when I was in fourth grade. I wore it on a trip to a state park with my parents and my brother. I was walking ahead of everyone, and I remember feeling my father's eyes on my back in my new low-cut bathing suit. Did he think I looked sexy? I hoped so. The back was cut all the way down to just above my bottom. I didn't have breasts yet, but some of the girls in my class did. I was looking forward to getting mine. I remember going off the path and into the greenery to pull down my shorts and then my bathing suit to pee. The stream splashed up on my shoes. I wondered if my father was peeking at me. Sometimes I caught him looking at me when I was doing things. Not expecting to be watched, and finding him watching me. One time I was shitting and I was looking down through my legs and trying to watch the shit come out and fall into the water. Then I looked up and saw my father's legs right in front of me. I didn't like that. He wasn't supposed to watch me shit.

I went up into the sky. Up, up, all the way up, and I looked down and saw a little girl and her father. Her legs were spread. His cock was going into her. He was piercing her with it. She had been wearing pink shorts, but her father pulled them off her, and her underwear, too. Her shirt had a hedgehog on it. It was from a nature center in England that her aunt had visited. She didn't have breasts yet. She was maybe eight or nine.

Sometimes I read my father's journals without him knowing. When I was a teenager, one time I read that nothing felt as good to him as being naked around me. Another time he wrote that little girls can be so sexy because they just love you and they want you to touch them.

When Richard Serra was a boy, he was standing on the shore and he watched an old ship get launched into the sea. This gargantuan thing was set into the water, where it made the water move like mad, but the water held it. He says he thinks that all of his work might be about that day—about the transfer of mass and heavy things being buoyed up.

Maybe all of the things I do are about my father raping me before I knew how to read or write.

There is a fairy tale called "The Girl Without Hands" in which a daughter cuts off her own hands to make herself grotesque so that her father will no longer want to marry her. My aunt Karen covers herself in ever-increasing rolls of fat. Her body is enormous from grief. She consumes and consumes and consumes. I think it's her way both to hide her pain and her shame and to retroactively repel the advances of her grandfather. She is my father's younger sister, and their grandfather Paul molested them both. Karen and I can't talk about any of it. Eating with her is like being with a lion and her kill. Kill her pain with sugar, kill her body with fat. She wants to be grotesque. I didn't and I don't want to be grotesque.

It didn't hurt when my father rubbed my pussy with his fingers, or when I rubbed my pussy on his leg. Those things felt good. I liked it when he masturbated. I liked it because it was exciting for me to watch. Sometimes he rubbed the tip of his penis along my pussy and that felt good, too. He liked looking down at his penis rubbing me. I liked looking, too. I liked the feel of his flesh rubbing my flesh. Putting his cock into me was pure pain until my body was big enough, which wasn't until I was a teenager. I remember being afraid it would hurt the way it had before—like I was being torn, split in two, blood everywhere, but suddenly it didn't. My body was finally big enough; I was wet, too. I must have been fourteen or so. I remember being naked on a foam mattress on the floor of one of the houses my father lived in after he left my mother. We were alone then, except for my brother. We hid from him just as we had hid from my mother, from the world. I remember the feeling of my body getting fucked on that foam mattress. There wasn't a mattress pad—just a cotton sheet over the yellow foam—and it didn't feel good to move on it. But it felt good when he was inside me finally—now that I was big enough. I had little breasts, too. It was different. My body was so much bigger and I was shy and covered my breasts while we did it. I remember those dark days full of light when my father fucked me.

I remember years before—when I was little—feeling my wet pussy. My fleshy little pussy lips. He touched them with his large fingers; he liked the way it felt. I had orgasms. I remember how scary they felt. Scary and so good. Like I was flying and falling and exploding and about to die. I didn't know if my body would still be there when it was over. Every time he fucked me, every time he made himself come, or me come, I was pushed further into solitude.

I remember his sounds. His breathing, heavy and fast, trying to be quiet, trying to be quiet while his cock was so hard and he just had to, he had to rub it between my thighs. I remember his low moaning. I remember looking into his mouth. His mouth agape and tense as he rubbed his penis, looking down at it, rubbing it, getting more excited by looking at his penis with its wet red head.

All things are lawful for me. (The Apostle Paul)

I can see his face, his blue eyes, his white hair. I see his clean-shaven face. I can see his eyes like beams driving into me. They drive through my clothes and see all of my nakedness. Me as a child, me as a teenager, me as a woman.

When I was in first grade, I took half of a plastic Easter egg and put it in my underwear so that it looked like I had a little bulging penis. I touched the hard egg in my underwear. I touched it and I rubbed it and I made myself excited rubbing my hard little dick egg.

I don't know if this is accurate, but the feeling I have, and always had, is that really my father wanted to kill me but that I seduced him to keep him from killing me. I became sexy to keep myself alive. I saved my life by giving him sexual pleasure. And he became addicted to our sex, and then I did, too. Or maybe he really wanted to harm himself, so he caused me pain in order to feel his own pain. He destroyed himself by causing me pain, but that gave him pleasure. I read about a man who murdered his wife because he said that was the only way he could kill himself.

Several years ago, I fell in love with a man named Carl. At first I thought he was gentle, but another part of me smelled his violence. And he smelled my fear, like a dog. He smelled my need for violence, which I didn't recognize that I had. One night, he demanded that I tell him that he owned me. His eyes were other. He was angry and I was frightened. But my reaction was not to run away. Sometimes I feel safer when I'm very, very still, barely breathing. My body became aroused, I was exceedingly wet, my body wanted safety. All I wanted to do was have sex with him to calm him down, to protect myself. I wanted to have sex with him all night until the sun came up, when I could be protected by the light of day instead. And then the following night, I wanted it to happen again. I asked him if he owned me, and he said yes. He told me that my body was made for him to fuck.

In moments when he really frightened me, it took only a few minutes for me to come from his fingers, his cock, his tongue. The more I actually feared harm by him, the more excited I felt, the more deeply bonded I felt to him.

During dinner when my brother and I were kids, it was a frequent occurrence for my mother to sit down, take one bite, and then say she wasn't feeling well and get up from the table and withdraw to her bedroom. She was very thin and rarely did we see her eat well.

When I was very young, my mother said we couldn't afford red meat, real Parmesan cheese, or real maple syrup. We shopped for clothes in thrift stores that smelled like sour dairy. I remember passing stores and seeing brand-new little dresses and wanting one, but my mother said no. Yet my mother always had her horses. And my grandparents who lived in London paid for private school for my brother and me. I don't know how my mother paid for her horses or steeplechasing. My parents didn't drink alcohol because it was too expensive. We turned out the lights every time we left a room, and in the winter we were cold. We ate meat only on special occasions. It was the Parmesan and the meat that I wanted. I didn't care about missing going to the movies, but I desperately wanted real maple syrup and beef.

I lied to the children in my class and told them my family was rich. Wealth was equated with purity, safety, and good in my little brain. One day I had my friend Julie over to play. She saw my house. She knew we weren't allowed to go into my parents' bedroom, where my mother was in bed. She knew we had to be quiet so as not to bother her. Julie saw the things that we had in our small house. The chair with the stuffing popping out. The rickety yellow table with cat food and a bleeding heart plant on top. She saw that we were poor, not rich. She didn't mind, but I didn't want her to come over anymore, I preferred going to her enormous, clean house.

Years later, around the time my father left my mother, when I was ten, he began to make more money. And then, when I was thirteen, his father gave him and his sister a living trust. So during my teenage years, my father bought me things and I was able to do things that my mother couldn't. I went out to fancy restaurants with friends when I was fourteen. I told her about how soft and sweet tuna toro was. I bought myself expensive shoes. Shoes and dresses she told me made me look like a hooker.

When we had fights about things and money, I reminded her about her horses, about the expenses, the vet bills that were sometimes thousands of dollars. I told her that it was all right for us to like different things. I wanted pretty shoes. And I wanted to travel. She said she couldn't afford to travel. When I told her that if she wanted to travel she could choose to, she would get so angry at me that she would throw things at my head.

Then she would cry. She wanted a daughter, but she didn't want me for a daughter.

As a teenager, I had recurring nightmares about my bloody insides being everywhere. Getting caught in my own intestines. Finding my dismembered parts in the street, in public buildings, hanging from trees. I used to terrify my friends when I spent the night at their houses by screaming in the night, and sometimes I told them about these dreams. I thought it was normal for girls to have dreams like that. But they didn't have those same dreams of walking through a city park and looking down, and where the green grass had just been were now bloody uteruses, vaginas, guts, lungs, wet pink brains sloshing around underfoot. And up in the trees, my decapitated head, my poked-out eyes, my long-haired scalp hanging from a blossoming tree branch.

For a long time, I couldn't have an orgasm without seeing my father's face. It was his white hair and his piercing blue eyes that I used to see when I came. The horror of seeing his face, and of that being the image that made me come, was overwhelmingly disturbing, and it also made me deeply excited. As if my ultimate erotic experience is being raped by the man who created me. His lust and his force infected my own desire.

A couple times a year, I have a dream where it's just him and me in the world. Finally just the two of us, and we can fuck all we want. I wake up nauseated and dizzy.

I didn't touch myself ever when I was a teenager. When I was alone, I was frightened of my body, of what it could do, of pleasure.

But one day in college, I was sitting and reading on top of one of the basement washing machines in my dorm, waiting for the wash cycle to be done. The vibration felt good. I reached down and touched my pussy while the washing machine whirred. I didn't come there in the basement, but I did later that night in my bed. I felt the same terror and thrill that I felt when I had orgasms as a girl. And then it started. I masturbated all the time throughout my early twenties and during the first few years that I was married. I couldn't stop. I did it everywhere I could. I did it in bed every night and in the shower and on long drives and in airplanes. I rubbed myself with my ring and middle fingers. I imagined myself as a nine- or ten-year-old girl—just before getting breasts—seducing men, strange men, grotesque men, holding their cocks, sucking them, making them fuck me, filling myself with them, their hands pressing hard on my flat child's chest while they thrust into me. Sometimes the men wore masks, and sometimes the men were animals. Sometimes they covered my mouth, sometimes I watched them fuck other girls.

When I was in first grade, my favorite pants were purple corduroy. One day, I shit my purple pants. I wouldn't use the bathroom at school, and I had diarrhea in my pants. It reeked of rotten fish. I remember how hot my cheeks were with the shame. The shame blossomed red in my cheeks. The kids made faces and held their noses at the terrible smell I'd made. Miss Katie called my mother and said I was sick and to please come pick me up. My mother put a towel over the seat where I sat in the car.

I wasn't sick.

One day, my father found me looking at *The Joy of Sex*. I was sitting on the floor of my parents' bedroom looking at a picture of a Japanese woman on a swing—sitting so that her huge, furled, pink vagina was exposed. A man with an erection was waiting in line with the swing so that he would penetrate her when she swung into him. My father screamed at me when he found me sitting on the floor looking at that book. He said that book was only for adults and I was a very bad girl for looking at the book I found on his bedside table.

One night my father came into my room after I fell asleep and got into my bed. He clutched my sleeping body and woke me up with his penis between my butt cheeks—back and forth and back and forth—then jammed it inside me, my entire body being fucked by this enormous thing displacing my organs, making my vision blur as if his penis were going all the way up, all the way through me, up my rib cage, as if it would shoot out of my mouth, or go into my brain. That's how it felt, like being impaled on a huge, thrusting spike. He was putting his penis inside me like those people I saw in the book—doing things only for grown-ups to do—and I knew my father was a liar.

I wasn't sick either when I stayed home for two months in the fourth grade with a mysterious illness. I had symptoms like dizziness, muscle aches, sharp stomach pains and no energy or desire to leave the house. My parents took me to all kinds of doctors and they all said I was fine. When it was just the two of us, my father angrily said he knew I wasn't really sick.

I stayed home alone every day, and when I got lonely I picked up our rotary phone and called the bank number, which had a recording of the time and temperature. I liked listening to the woman's robotic voice.

In ballet, every time I spread my legs I was worried other people would know. Would they see what I did at night? One day at my grandmother's house, I lay on my back and held my little brother in the air over me with my legs, playing airplane. My grandmother startled me by walking in the room when I thought she was outside in her garden. I was so worried that she would know that I had sex. That she would be able to tell from how I lay on the floor on my back with my legs in the air. And could she tell that I liked sex?

Every time I spread my legs, I felt things going up inside me. Sharp things, hard things, body parts, toys, animals, car parts, skyscrapers. I fought with my mind to get things out of my body. But my body still feels it.

When I was eight years old, we moved to a new house. I assumed the master bedroom was for me and my father and that my mother would sleep in one of the other bedrooms. I had a count in my head of how many times my parents had had sex. This was very important to me. I hated them for having sex with each other. The number in my head was five. One for each time they conceived a child, and the three times that I had caught my father on top of my mother. His buttocks moved and clenched as he drove what was mine into her. I never wanted them to have sex again. I wanted them to separate. Two years later, they did.

The mulberry trees were fruiting when we moved in. There was so much fruit we didn't know what to do with it. The berries fell onto the ground and got stuck on the bottoms of my feet when I played outside. I made berry stains on the wood floors and my mother made me clean them with a rag.

While we were in that house, my mother went down to Virginia on a horse trip of some kind. I sent her a card and on the front of it I drew a little girl with a cobra snake coming out of her mouth. My mother still has the card. She thinks it's sweet.

One of my father's aunts drowned herself. One of her daughters, a girl named Jacqueline, was a teenager when she got up from the table where she was having Christmas supper with her family and excused herself, and then they heard a bang. I told that story to the beautiful therapist and she said that it is unusual for a girl to use a gun.

In the master bedroom at our new house, something happened when my mother was away in Virginia. My father was threatening to hang himself. He was standing with a coarse, thick sisal rope around his neck. He was wearing a white T-shirt and gray athletic pants. He was barefoot. I was in a dress. A pale orange dress. I can see myself because I saw it from above. My hair, still blond, was up in barrettes. I wanted to save him. He was killing himself because of me. It was my fault. I put my hand on his crotch. My face was at the height of his crotch. He wasn't wearing underwear. I stroked him the way I had watched him do to himself standing over my bed at night. I told him not to hurt himself. With the rope still around his neck he pulled down his pants and let me touch his bare skin. His penis was hard and up now, and his eyes were softer. We both used our hands on his penis. We touched and rubbed his penis standing there in the late afternoon until he came into his hand. Then he went into the bathroom to wash it off before he took the rope off his neck. I remember the outline of his penis in his athletic pants after he pulled them back up. I don't know whether he could have really hanged himself in that room, I don't know if there was anything strong enough or high enough, but, then, I believed that he could and was relieved when he took the rope back to the garage. I remember him stroking my head and squeezing the back of my neck hard when he came.

We rolled the Christmas cookie dough out thin on pastry cloths with my mother's big rolling pin. We got down the tin full of cookie cutters and we cut out deer and bells and rabbits and Santa Clauses. Hearts and owls and angels and little houses. We decorated the cutout cookies with colorful sprinkles and silver balls. My mother was happy the days before Christmas.

She would put felt antlers on Stradivarius and Hookah. My brother and I dressed up like Santa Claus and rode the horses around to the neighbors' houses. We ended up at the house across the road from ours, where everyone would gather for carols and eggnog.

We made holly wreaths. We made gingerbread houses. We put real candles on the big Christmas tree. We set up Nativity scenes in various little spots around the house. I loved the ceramic, wood, straw, and china Holy Families, wise men, and animals. I thought baby Jesus was beautiful. I loved that he was conceived without sex.

My mother wasn't happy on Christmas Day itself—but the days up to it were filled with joy, cheer, and excitement. On Christmas Day she was sad. I don't know why. I never understood her sadness. Why she would get up from the table in the middle of dinner and burst into tears and go to her room and shut the door.

At the new house, there was a big climbing tree. It was a maple that I named King Henry. I remember filo dough in the freezer. I used to eat it cold. It was like eating paper. My brother played with trucks. I did ballet. The neighborhood girls didn't like me. One day I put a jingle bell inside myself. I took out the bell and smelled my pussy on the metal.

I remember my father's green bathrobe. And his dark green slippers. I remember his white hair messy in the morning, his blue eyes, his scratchy face. He was on the bed in the master bedroom. Lying on top of the covers in his bathrobe, surrounded by the newspaper. His robe was open and he had no underwear. I went into the room. It was just us in the house. I don't know where my mother and brother were. I could see his large testicles between his legs and the open green robe. His penis wasn't hard yet. He told me to climb up on the bed. I did, and I climbed on the newspaper. He pushed my head down with his hand to rest it on his belly. My head was there, with my ear near his belly button. I could hear the sounds of his digestion, and I saw his flaccid penis and his testicles. He rubbed, he touched them, he played with his penis. It started getting bigger. It got big and it got bigger. He was playing with my hair while his left hand ran up and down his cock, which was dancing as it got harder, dancing as he played with it. He asked me to lick it. Lick it and suck on it. He put his right hand inside my nightgown. Inside my underwear. Underwear pulled down and off. And he took my nightgown off. He put his hand on my flat chest and rubbed the tip of his penis up and down my pussy. I was on all fours on top of him. He put his penis inside, not all the way up, but partway. He moved his hips and he moaned. He pushed on my head to make me move. Then we played with the cum. He rubbed it on my body and between his fingers. Stretchy gloopy eggwhite goo. I shouldn't have done that, he said, let's clean you up. I remember the stink of his coffee breath mixing with the sweet, bleachy smell of his semen.

Some of his cum got on the newspaper. The ink came off into the cum, making the liquid black. I squished the inky cum in my hand.

I remember that was the year we gave my father a new

bathrobe for his birthday. One with red checks. That year my teacher was Ms. Carleton. She spoke Italian. She taught us songs in Italian.

> *Il merlo ha perso la lingua*
> *come farà a cantar?*
> *Il merlo ha perso la lingua*
> *come farà a cantar?*
> *Il merlo ha perso la lingua,*
> *povero merlo mio, come farà a cantar?*

> The blackbird lost its tongue,
> How will it manage to sing?
> The blackbird lost its tongue,
> How will it manage to sing?
> The blackbird lost its tongue,
> My poor blackbird, how will it manage to sing?

Ms. Carleton desperately wanted a child of her own. She finally became pregnant. But the baby girl was stillborn. Ms. Carleton explained to our class about babies being born dead. The girl's name was Alice. Ms. Carleton cried telling us this story. I thought a lot about poor baby Alice Carleton, who didn't even get to live for one day.

———

Feeling hands on my neck and big fingers fingering me. Thinking of my fear. I can't help it. If I think about my father, the blood rushes between my legs.

I felt sorry for my pitiful father and my body made him feel better. This gave me an odd sense of my own power. I remember being asked by my high school friends how I would defend myself if a man attacked me and I readily replied that I would just have sex with the attacker to calm him down. I wasn't afraid of hijackers on airplanes the way my mother was, because in my mind, I would just have sex with them and they would stop hijacking the plane. I wasn't afraid of thieves the way my mother was because, again, I would fuck the thieves and they wouldn't steal from us.

I felt like I had something that my father wanted to take from me. I had something he didn't have, and he wanted it. I felt that way sometimes with other men later in my life. That they were trying to take something from me.

Climbing on my father, making his penis hard, made me feel powerful beyond feeling excited. Look what I could do. I could make this big strong man hard, and then he would rub it in my pussy, and I liked that and it was just us, just us in the world. Rubbing his big hard cock head in my little hairless pussy. He trusted me to do the right thing. And I did, I rubbed it and I held it throbbing in my little hands and I made him come.

When I was a little girl my father took me for Sunday drives. He made me a tree house. He brushed out the tangles in my hair.

Sex with my father made me an orphan.

I remember him cleaning the cum off of me with a paper towel before getting me dressed for school. I remember him ejaculating inside me when I was a teenager. My father may be crazy but he's not crazy; he wouldn't have risked getting me pregnant. He had a vasectomy sometime after my brother was born. Was it so he could fuck me?

Sometimes around cats I want to crush their skulls. But I never have and I never would. I did kill caterpillars, and once I wanted to hurt a little girl named Natalie. I killed the caterpillars with a rock and I watched the green and yellow ooze from their squished bodies. The little girl Natalie was the daughter of neighbors. When I was fifteen, they asked me to babysit. I walked down the road and across the field and over the hill to their dark, sad house and met the little girl. I don't know why, but I didn't like her at all. I wanted to harm her. I felt these things well up in my body. I wanted to tear her apart. I didn't want to be alone with that child for fear of myself. I was terrified of myself around that little girl, and I told her parents I didn't actually have time to babysit.

I babysat other children for whom I cared deeply. It was just that one—that little blond-haired, ugly girl—whom I wanted to injure.

Once, my parents had friends from out of town who came to stay with us. This was not long before my father left, but before we knew he was leaving. I was nine or ten years old. They had a daughter my age. I can't remember her name, but she was bigger than me and had long curly hair. She and I slept in the same bed. When she was asleep but I wasn't, I climbed on the girl who was my parents' friends' daughter and rubbed myself on her thigh. I pretended to French-kiss her and told her how pretty she was. She woke up with me riding her leg and whispering in her ear. She didn't seem to mind, in fact she liked it, and we continued. We pretended that I was a man and she was a girl. We did this for all of the nights they stayed. We never spoke to or saw each other again.

My mother's closest friend was an Indian woman named Lavanya. She and her husband, Charlie, lived in a three-story house with a big field out back with an old red McCormick tractor, which their daughter, Leela, and I played on sometimes. My mother and Lavanya would ride horses together, or spend afternoons whispering, huddled over teacups in the kitchen with the red table nestled into the gabled windows with duck-patterned fabric on the window seats. I remember, when I was very little, the two of them laughing one day at all the penises I drew. It made me ashamed and I stopped drawing penises. I didn't know that that was a funny or a surprising thing to do.

I liked playing with Leela. She and her family went to Bombay twice a year and brought back wonderful clothes and jewelry. We dressed up in her bright orange and blue and pink flowing saris, and painted red bindis between our eyes with her mother's Chanel lipsticks. We did dance performances in these clothes, and we played duets on the piano in the living room with some of her toy animals dressed up seated next to us. We had tea parties on the floor in their living room and we invited all her dolls.

Leela's father, Charlie, made wonderful food. I remember him toasting spices in a cast-iron pan to make garam masala. The cloves, the mustard seeds, the cardamom. Charlie made us Caesar salads, pastas, and grilled cheese sandwiches, too. Sometimes he would pretend to be a zombie and chase us around the house. One day he scolded us for dressing the cat in Leela's doll clothes and holding it down while we pushed it around in a toy perambulator.

I got my first period at their house. I was in the basement bathroom, the one with the mint-green tile from floor to ceiling and the chain on the toilet that you had to pull so hard to make it flush that I had to use both hands. Leela and I had been going through her mother's closet downstairs—the one with all the fancy dresses that she never wore anymore. We tried them on secretly, running to look at ourselves in the full-length mirror on the back of a door in the basement. Then running back and returning the dresses to their proper hangers in the zipped bags that smelled of mothballs and her mother's perfume.

I went to pee, and when I pulled my pale blue cotton underwear down to my ankles, I found a smear of red and brown blood. I thought I was dying. I didn't know what a period was. I told Leela that something was terribly wrong. She told me about menstruation and gave me a pad. I spent that night in Leela's trundle bed, and when I woke in the morning, there was a large bright red bloodstain on the sheet—my blood had leaked through the sanitary napkin. I remembered my grandmother saying to use cold water to remove stains from eggs or blood. I took the sheet and put it into the washing machine and turned it to cold and hoped that Lavanya wouldn't notice. I was embarrassed already, since Leela and I had gotten in trouble the day before for hitting the hanging bird feeder with badminton rackets.

When Lavanya drove me home in her old Land Rover, she asked me if I had gotten my period before. I said no. My face was red with shame. She pulled out three sanitary napkins from her purse and handed them to me. "Welcome," she said. She told me to talk to my mother about it. But I didn't. It was my father who bought me menstrual pads of different kinds and sizes. Regular, overnight, panty liners. With wings and without.

I have a friend whose father was violent, but not sexually violent. When my friend David was eight years old, his father beat him for getting a poor grade in math. David knew that his father kept a handgun in his bedroom closet. That night, while his father slept, David snuck into the closet, found the gun, and went to his father's bedside. He aimed the gun at his father's head. He wanted to kill him. He stood there for some time, holding the gun, prepared to kill his father. But he couldn't do it. He returned the gun to the closet and went back to bed.

After that, David stopped eating meat. The reason was, when he was holding the gun aimed at his father, he felt his own violence and he felt the strong desire to kill him. But he didn't want to be a killer. He was afraid, though, of his desire to kill. This, anyway, is the answer he gave me when I asked him at a restaurant why he became a vegetarian.

The day my father left us I stopped eating meat. I was ten years old. We ate it more often in those days. Meat was my favorite thing to eat. I needed to deprive myself of something I didn't want to live without. I remember that my mother cooked bacon the first morning my father was gone. I adored bacon, but I told her I was no longer eating meat. She didn't think it would last beyond a day, then a week. But then years went by and I refused to touch or to eat meat. When asked why, I told people that it was for environmental reasons, but that was a lie. And I wasn't afraid of my desire to kill. I was afraid of my desire to have sex with my father.

I didn't eat meat for several years. Until one evening when my father and I were at a restaurant and he ordered us both New York strip steaks. I reminded him that I didn't eat meat, and he said it was time to start again. I ate the meat, and then I threw it up in the bathroom. A few days later, I tried meat again and I didn't throw up.

From the time I was very young, my father told me that we were one person, that I was just a part of him. I grew up with that inside me. I grew up with him inside me.

I feel his pleasure exploding out of me. His pleasure between my legs. I want to fuck myself like that, feel him splitting me in two. Feeling us become each other and something else entirely.

Is this a love story? It's a creation story.

After my father left my mother, he moved around a lot. I remember the house with the yellow foam mattress on his bedroom floor. I remember the house with the leaking roof and the white mildewed shower curtain in the bathroom. And later, the house near a pond. It was in the house near the railroad tracks where I was very concerned about the Persian Gulf War. I wrote letters to President Bush. I wrote letters to soldiers. I read Herodotus and Henry Miller and Flaubert. I won the prize for most promising young science student. My teachers were thoughtful and asked me to talk about how I was feeling about my parents' divorce. I said I was fine. I wore white collared shirts and pink, navy-blue, forest-green, and black cardigans. I wore black skirts and my hair up in a twist. I didn't pay attention to the boys. I had two close girlfriends, and I did my homework. I got my period for the first time and I finally had breasts big enough for a bra. I played tennis.

In my English class in eighth grade, we were required to keep a daily journal that was reviewed once a week by our teacher, Ms. Olinski. After a couple of months she called me into her office after school. I was so afraid I had done something wrong. "No, no, dear, you are doing wonderfully. But why haven't you once mentioned something about yourself in your diary?" I wrote about only two things: daily details of the Persian Gulf War and the weather. I wrote about the war and the weather and I described them in detail every day.

The curves of the clouds, where they were white and where they had gray. If the gray was from shadows, or if it was from being full of rain and the clouds were about to burst. I wrote about the color of the sky. Whether it was hazy or blue. What kind of blue in the morning, what kind of blue at noon, and the blue before the sunset. And the blue of dark, of night, and the moon. Waxing or waning. I wrote about the shadows of the clouds on the fields. I wrote about birds. I wrote about how the air smelled. I wrote about dust, I wrote about wind. I wrote about how the smell of the rain hitting the earth was like yellow mustard.

One night, in the house with the leaky roof, my father asked me to watch the movie *The Name of the Rose*. He asked me to pay particular attention to the sex scene and tell him how it made me feel. Did I like how that wild peasant girl seduced the boy? Did I like the squealing sounds she made? Yes, I did.

One day, at Leela's house when we were teenagers, we made sandwiches to take on a picnic. Her father, Charlie, taught us to sprinkle salt, pepper, and a little oregano on the tomato in the sandwiches. We didn't do that at my house. It made the sandwiches taste so good. On our picnic, I asked Leela if her father ever asked her, when they were in public, if people thought she was his young girlfriend or his daughter. She replied that maybe it had crossed her father's mind at some point, but it wasn't something that he would ever say.

Charlie also taught us how to roast red peppers. To cook them at four hundred degrees, until the skins turn brown and black and make popping sounds. Put them in a plastic bag and let them cool. Then peel off the skins, slice the peppers, and place them in a bowl with olive oil and minced garlic. He said you can add a pinch of salt or not.

I liked very much to be in their company, and it made me feel lonely. To be around a father and a daughter who loved each other very much, who teased each other and enjoyed each other. A father who wanted the best for his daughter. A father who was a father and a daughter who was nothing more than a daughter.

Leela lost her virginity to a wonderful boy. I know he was a wonderful boy because he was the first boy I kissed. He wanted me to be his girlfriend. I was fifteen years old. But after a few weeks, I had to tell him I couldn't see him anymore. How can you have a boyfriend when you have a father like mine? You can't. Then he and Leela started dating, and then having sex. I never spoke to him again. I was afraid of my own desire and I felt desire around him and that made me feel ashamed. I avoided him at school. If I saw he sat in a particular chair, I never sat in that chair again. I didn't want to touch anything he touched. I started washing my hands too much again. Washing them until they bled.

In high school there was a boy who wanted to suck my tongue. He was the son of the man who offered me one of his luxury cars if I let him fist-fuck me. It happened at his son's sixteenth-birthday party. The man came over to me on his terrace, held my elbow, and whispered the offer in my ear. His son had shown me and other friends his father's beautiful cars, old and new. Gray, dark green, dark blue, white, and black. Was the offer real? I don't know, but it felt serious. I was intrigued by both the father and the son. I didn't let the father fist-fuck me in exchange for a car. I felt desire, but I liked feeling pure even more. Purity with rare interruptions of deviousness. Purity in those days was doing very well in school. Purity was memorizing dates of historical significance. The Battle of Hastings. The year Machiavelli wrote *The Prince.* The birth of Johann Sebastian Bach. The year that Caravaggio painted *The Seven Acts of Mercy.*

Deviousness in those days was letting that boy suck my tongue when I should have been in chemistry class.

Mrs. Martin came and spoke to our eleventh-grade health class. She came to talk about child abuse. She had been molested by an uncle. She came to talk about the abuse of power. She came to talk about harm caused to children. It is the only time I have ever fainted in my life. I fainted when she said the word *incest*. I felt dizzy and ill afterward. Mrs. Martin came over and kindly asked me if anything had ever happened to me. I told her that my piano teacher French-kissed me once. Which is true, but that was nothing. Just a disgusting man putting his tongue in my mouth. It tasted like peanut butter.

Mrs. Martin told me that whatever happened wasn't my fault. The health teacher told me I was excused to go home.

That day, I was wearing a light blue floral sundress with buttons all the way up. It was the same dress that I wore years later on the night I was date-raped. Because I went to the emergency room, the hospital was required to take my clothing for DNA testing, should I choose to press charges. They told me they would keep my blue sundress and my flower bra for ten years in frozen storage. I asked them if I could get my clothes back after ten years, because I really liked that dress, and they said, unfortunately no, the evidence would be incinerated. A few years ago was the ten-year mark. I thought about my sundress and my bra. I imagined a city employee going through the drawers in frozen storage and pulling out my clothes and dropping them into an incinerator.

After my father left my mother, my mother never dated or remarried, but devoted herself more and more to steeplechasing. My father had girlfriends. I liked it that he had girlfriends, and I happened to like them, too. You might think I would be jealous, but I wasn't. It was a relief. I especially liked Gloria. She was lovely. She was an economist. She gardened in a black cocktail dress and she drank a split of champagne every night. She told me that her favorite thing to eat for supper when she was by herself was crackers and cheese. One night when we ate hamburgers at her house, she used her best china and her damask napkins. I wanted her and my father to get married, which they spoke about at one point. But they didn't. The last time I saw her was at my grandmother's funeral when she left trace lipstick marks on both of my cheeks.

Going into my father's room while he was taking a nap. He woke up from the sound of the door. He was sleepy. He raised the covers to invite me in. He wasn't hard just then, but a few minutes later he was, after I put my hand on his penis. After I felt it grow and stiffen in my hands. Then he slipped it inside me. I was wet from it hardening in my hands. Wet from being under those covers where I felt so disgusted. After we both came, I got up and left.

After I had an orgasm, I wanted to be as far away from him as I could. It made me want to disappear, to vanish into the air. I went to do my homework. I was writing a paper on the Renaissance.

André Breton wrote that Frida Kahlo's paintings are like pretty ribbons tied on bombs. I love the paintings she did of her body being hurt. The ones where her skin is pierced by nails, arrows, thorns. Her body in bed, covered in blood and wounds. Snipping her own veins. She was wounded by a metal pole impaling her pelvis. But she was fierce and she survived. Her paintings made my body feel, they made my body scream.

I made copies of her paintings as self-portraits when I was a teenager. I was a terrible painter, but I liked doing it. I made myself an easel and I looked at myself in the mirror. I painted my face and my hair. I painted my eyes and I painted my lips. I painted monkeys on my shoulders with soft black fur. I painted thorns piercing my neck just like she did. I painted tears. I painted a man in my forehead. The man in her forehead is Diego. The man in my forehead was my father. He liked my paintings. I painted the Prudential Tower in Boston impaling my pelvis. I hung my paintings on the wall of my new room at my father's new house. He didn't fuck me in that room. But he did fuck me in his bedroom, when I went in to him. He let me lead the way.

One ribbon was green and one was pink. He used a steak knife. I don't know why he did any of this. He tied me to the chair and he spread my legs and put the knife inside and he cut. I was eight or nine years old. It was just my father and me alone in my parents' bedroom. I was so afraid, and deep inside my fear I went soft. I don't know how to explain it. I was so uncomfortable and so frightened that it made me light. I floated up out of that bedroom and house. I lived in the sky. I played in the clouds. My body was down in that house, but I was up in the sky. I *was* the sky. I was endless blue sky when I was tied to the chair when he put the knife inside and cut.

Inside the house with the leaky roof, it reeked of mold and must. It got into everything. My clothes, my hair stank of must. My father said he was sorry we lived there, and he would slip money into my schoolbag and tell me to buy something nice. Soon we would move, he said. My father cried a lot and said how sorry he was that he had failed in the marriage to my mother. His sadness and that disgusting house made me want to fuck him. I wanted to make him feel better. I felt bigger than him, like I could and should take care of him.

I remember the house full of buckets in a rainstorm. The water splashed on the thick brown carpet. My father was on his foam mattress on the floor saying how sorry he was that we didn't live in a better house. I got into bed with him. He felt better.

The legacy of incest in my family is long. My father told me that he and his younger sister were molested by their grandfather Paul. My brother has Paul's original wristwatch, which Louis Cartier himself made for the Brazilian aviator Santos-Dumont, who, for a brief while, was thought to be the first man to fly. I have two things from my great-grandfather Paul: a silver crucifix that says *Semper Fidelis*—the marines' motto—and the legacy of the use of small children for sex.

My father's mother was raped by her father, the same Paul. She told me about it when she was dying. She wanted to talk. She had always kept things to herself, but now she was desperate to talk. She said that she got her cancer from keeping everything in. She told me not to worry about making mistakes in life, that everyone does, but don't *ever* be overweight.

She ate one strip of bacon with peaches for breakfast

every morning. She always had two greyhounds—Roger and Betsy. The names stayed the same, but the dogs changed. She collected rocks. Everywhere she went—from Nebraska to the Seychelles—she took away a rock. Some were small and some were quite large. She confessed to me that she really loved Curtis, the man she met in her reading group. They read *The History of the Decline and Fall of the Roman Empire*, and Virgil and Homer in their original Latin and Greek. My grandmother was close to Curtis's wife. Curtis adored my grandmother. He and his wife had been friends of my grandparents, and they and other couples went on tours together. They went to Egypt and Tibet, to Sri Lanka, Namibia, Mexico, Japan. Curtis's wife died, and at one point my grandfather was very occupied with his work, but my grandmother still went on the trips and so did Curtis. This went on for many years, my grandmother told me. And sometimes it was complicated. He bought her jewelry that she wore only when she was away from her husband. And years into it, Curtis would beat the shit out of her. Leave her with emeralds at her throat and sapphires on her fingers in a battered pile at the bottom of the stairs.

She told me she loved Curtis. She loved him and she forgave him. She hid their affair, but she couldn't always explain away the marks. For a graceful, athletic woman it just didn't make sense that she was always bumping into things with her face or accidentally falling down the stairs. She said she was heartbroken when she heard that Curtis had died rather unexpectedly. And the heartbreak was made worse by the fact that she had to mourn him in secret.

I told her to eat yogurt. I told her it had a lot of calcium and she needed calcium. I wanted so badly for her to live. She told me that cancer was the best thing that ever happened to her. It made everything clear. All the fights she'd had with herself for so long were over. But I wanted her to live.

One night, she lifted up her purple nightgown and showed me the scars on her flat chest. I rubbed her feet while she told me that she wasn't going to say goodbye to me. She was going to say goodbye to everyone else who came to see her, but she wanted me to tell her that I loved her, and then to get up and walk out of her room and not look back.

I was seventeen and applying to college. I told her I was going to spend a year abroad in Chile. "That's nice," she said. She suggested that I read up on Darwin.

It is rare for me to lose or misplace things. But every piece of jewelry I had from her, I lost. Most of her jewelry came from Curtis. Maybe my body thought about him every time I put on her delicate platinum choker. The gold in my ears. The pearls at my throat. All of it is gone. In college, I used to wear the choker all the time, and one morning I felt my neck and it was gone. Her pearls slipped off my neck, too, down my blouse, and into the snow on a walk through wintry Boston. Every time it happened, I thought she was telling me something.

I was angry when my father told me about watching her when he was young. My father would spy on his mother and watch her undress—he said he was excited by her beautiful and full breasts. He told me that he remembers a particular time when she had a white apron around her waist, but she was topless—no shirt and no bra. He was peeking at her from behind a door. He watched her breasts wobble when she moved. He said she was never more beautiful.

At her funeral, my father turned to me and said he would no longer be able to speak to me. He said that he didn't know for how long, but I reminded him too much of her.

I felt shocked, but I also felt relief. My grandmother—his mother—was the only decent thing binding us together. When his mother was alive, we spent so many long hours talking about her. I wanted to talk more to keep him from having sex with me. And now, with her gone, we had nothing to talk about. Which meant that sex was closer. The conversation stops, and it's just us and our two bodies. And I felt the desire from him for what he really wanted from me. He wanted my body. In my darkness I wanted him, too, but in my heart I didn't want him to ever touch me again.

My brother and I can talk about our mother. We talk about what a terrible houseguest she is. She can't help it. She is uncomfortable in houses that aren't her own, and she injures herself, and knocks into things, and doesn't want to do the activities we suggest doing. She sleeps in till noon, and wants to have breakfast when others are having lunch. It seems like every time she washes the dishes, she breaks a glass and cuts herself, which my brother is convinced is her way of getting out of doing any more dishes. She takes things out of the refrigerator and doesn't put them back. She bends my silver teaspoons by digging into hard ice cream to have just one small taste. We talk about how thin she is, how we worry that she doesn't eat enough. But we can't even mention our father.

I remember the house my father lived in near a pond. I remember the softness of the air outside that house. For the first time, my brother and I had our own big bed-rooms. I remember the light sky up above the heavy, wet air. This was one of the first times my father spoke to me again after my grandmother died. I was just about to leave for Chile. He was drinking white wine. There was a wood engraving of two figures and a moon and a tree over his bed that had belonged to my grandmother. There was a branch over the moon. The figures were plump and in silhouette. The man wore a hat, the woman a long dress. The green blanket on my father's bed had a hole in it. I woke up in that bed. I don't remember how or when I got there. I was cold. He was sipping his white wine, turning the pages of his book. I was naked, I had goose bumps. He pulled the green blanket over me. The hole passed over my body as the blanket was pulled up. He covered my head. I moved down so that I could look through the hole. The hole over my eye where I could peek out and see the white ceiling fan. I watched the still fan while something went in my pussy.

That blanket with a hole, a hole to embarrass me, to mock me. A hole to excite me. A hole to make me a woman. Like an Orthodox matrimonial sheet. A hole only for something to go through it, all the rest is to be hidden. All of me was to be hidden. A confessional blanket. I'm talking through the hole in the blanket and all you can see is my mouth. I don't remember exactly what happened that afternoon. But I feel something binding my wrists, and I can still smell the nauseating scent of his white wine. I hear the turning pages of his book. I remember the embarrassing and sexy feeling of my nipple popping out of the hole in the dark green blanket. And the engraved branch over the moon. With my eyes closed, I saw the dark branch cutting the bright moon in half.

Once, I went on a trip alone to visit colleges. I stayed with my cousin Martha in her dorm room at Harvard. I took the train to Providence one day and to Philadelphia another. I went into New York and interviewed at Columbia. That trip was not long after my grandmother had died.

The fall before she died, my father took me to look at colleges. Princeton, Bryn Mawr, Wellesley. I was sixteen, with my hair up in a ponytail. I wore a denim skirt, denim jacket. A white V-neck shirt and simple black shoes. I remember holding my legs closed tightly as we drove. I remember being aware of my father's eyes looking at my bare legs coming out of my skirt. I crossed my arms across my chest as he drove. I remember feeling very tense and trying not to be sexy. But it didn't matter. It was just the two of us. I remember being at a small restaurant and he ordered a bottle of wine and snuck me some. It felt like being on a date. He leaned in to talk to me softly. I remember his blue eyes in the candlelight. He told me he'd never felt as close to anyone as he felt to me. That he didn't like talking to anyone as much as me.

Driving in the car. I don't like it, because I didn't like it, but I felt desire when he asked me to suck his cock. I did it and it excited me. Is it the same as Vietnam veterans getting excited when discussing the violence of war? I'm excited writing this, the way a man is excited talking about a battle.

When we were alone, we were a couple. It didn't matter how much I tried to be a daughter, I wasn't. We shared a hotel room. We slept in separate beds as we should have, but I sucked my father's cock that day while we drove. I felt his cock all the way down my throat. I swallowed his spurts of cum. He was wearing a green-and-white-checked shirt.

He threatened to kill himself if I told anyone.

My mother's mother told me I was a bad girl when I came home late one night in high school when she was visiting us. I wasn't a bad girl. I had been studying at the library and then at my friend Jessica's house.

When it was just the two of us, I told her that my father raped me. She didn't say anything. She was quiet for a minute or two before she asked me if I would like a tuna fish sandwich. That is the moment I felt like a very bad girl.

After I graduated from high school, I won a scholarship to spend a year abroad. I went to Chile and lived there with a family. They had three small children who told me I wore funny clothes and thought it was weird that I wanted to eat eggs for breakfast. I attended school in Spanish and French. I traveled as much as I could—from the Atacama Desert, where the Milky Way looked like a giant, pulsing umbilical cord, to the San Rafael Glacier, to Magdalena Island in the Strait of Magellan. I went to the Pomerape volcano with a few other international students, and it made me uncomfortable because it had the word *rape* in it. It was a word I did not like to ever say. But I also didn't fear rape. I don't know how to explain that disconnect. One day, I spent the afternoon with girls from my class after school, and one girl asked us all what our biggest fear was. Every single girl replied *rape*. When it got to me, I said without thinking about it, "Don't worry, it's not so bad, just pretend you like it so you can survive." They all looked at me and no one said anything. It made them forget that I hadn't said what my biggest fear was.

I went to the skiing towns in the Andes where a few infamous Nazis still lived near the million acres of land that, legend had it, Hitler still legally owned. An old woman at a pharmacy where I went to buy sunscreen one day told me that after World War II ended, Hitler lived and died in Chile on an island named Friendship.

I went to see the whales breeding in Puerto Madryn with my school class, and on the way back to Chile we stopped in Buenos Aires and saw the Casa Rosada. I traveled by bus. The buses are lovely—with reclining seats, and stewardesses who bring bread and butter and wine and pasta for dinner. Going south from the city you pass through grasslands with misty and soft air, the smeared landscape punctured by enormous cypress trees—majestic trees, holy trees. Polo horses and birds of prey.

My family's maid, Pascuala, was Quechua, originally from Peru. Pascuala lived in an apartment off the washroom in the garden. The washroom where she and Adelina—the maid who came every afternoon to help—washed and ironed the sheets and all the clothes. Pascuala didn't like me to walk around the house without a bra. She cleaned my shoes when I came home from school. She dusted my books and the little clock by my bed every day. She was very superstitious. One time she broke a mirror while she was cleaning it and then immediately walked to the lake to offer the pieces. It took her two days. We went out to dinner the nights she didn't cook for us—to a restaurant down the street with red-and-white-checked tablecloths. We ate fisherman's stew with red eel, which was the man of the house's favorite meal. I wasn't very close to the family I lived with, but we grew to be affectionate and they were always kind to me. It was the first time I felt like I was in the role of a daughter. The father, Juan Vicente, treated me like a daughter.

I had a room upstairs with pink floral wallpaper and a little bed with a dark blue bedspread. Out my window I looked down at a walled lawn below, and beyond that, the street. I watched the fruit-and-vegetable vendor across the street with his apron and his scale weighing things for the maids doing the morning shopping. And the farmers who came into town in the early hours with their donkey carts.

My father and my brother came to visit me for ten days. I remember the hotel in Santiago where I went to meet them, the yellow sheets. We shared a room. My brother was fifteen years old. I gave him his first cigarette on that trip—by a fountain on Santa Lucía Hill. My father slept in the bed next to ours and I remember waking up to the sound of him moaning. I looked over and saw him with the covers off and the silhouette of his penis in the air—and he was moving it, stroking it, moaning. My kind host family there kept saying how happy I must be to have my father and brother come visit. I watched my father in the bed next to us. He wrote in a notebook—journal entries—during that trip. He left the notebook open, and the next day before we went sightseeing, I read: *It feels so good to be naked with my children. In bed next to my children, feeling my sex with them sleeping soundly right next to me.*

After they left, I began to see a man. A man older than my father. A man who was tall and always wore three-piece suits. A man with a neatly trimmed beard and blue eyes just like my father's.

During a phone conversation with my father months later, he asked me if I had any love interests in Chile. I told him that I did. He asked me questions and I answered them. He asked me how old. Salvador was forty-nine. My father at the time was forty-six. I was eighteen. My father asked me about Salvador. What did this man do for a living? He was a businessman, but I didn't know what kind. Sometimes I waited in the car for him while he went to meetings. Had I had sex with this man? I had. Where? In hotels, in restaurant bathrooms, in his house when his wife was out. My father grew angry with the things I was telling him. He said, "Now that you're getting it from another man, you don't need me anymore." He hung up on me. He didn't call me again for the remainder of the months I was there.

When I returned home, my father took me out to dinner and asked me about Salvador. How did we meet? I told my father that, early one morning, I stopped in a café for a coffee on my walk to school. I asked the man reading the newspaper at the table next to me for the time, and after he told me, I jumped up because I was late. He offered to drive me so I wouldn't arrive late. As I got out of his car in front of the school, he said he would be there in the afternoon to pick me up.

I had seen his father playing chess at the cafés. His father, Honório, was a wily old man who liked to talk to me and my classmates after school. Honório claimed that his aristocratic Spanish mother died in childbirth, and that his *huaso* father hired a nanny, but she was not a wet nurse, so for comfort she put quince jam on her breasts for the infant Honório to suckle. Honório attributed his strength to having suckled jam instead of milk. He told us that he still ate quince jam on bread every evening before bed. Sometimes Honório's wife, Gerónima, would join him after her canasta games. When he told us his stories, she would roll her green eyes while she sipped her Campari.

I had seen Salvador before and he had seen me. I thought he was elegant and powerful. He said that he had noticed me and liked me because of the plain and modest clothes that I wore, and that I looked like a *paisana* from another place, another time, he told me the next morning when we met at the café again and he drove me to school. It began like this. We met at the café in the morning and he drove me to school. When the bell rang and the kids ran out of school at the end of the day, he was there waiting for me. He would drive me home. One day, after a week or so, he didn't go the usual way to my house. We went to a restaurant and he asked for a table in the back. We ate soup made of raw seafood. He put his hand on my thigh under the table and afterward we kissed in his car. The next evening we ate sea urchin and swordfish. Then we went for a drive afterward—he wanted to show me a view—and we were stopped at two roadblocks by military men with machine guns. As soon as Salvador rolled his window down, they nodded at him and waved us through. We had sex for the first time that night in the backseat of his car.

My father wanted to know more. I told him about driving to the top of a volcano in the middle of the night. I told him about Salvador showing me a *campamento*— one of the tent towns. I told my father about meeting Salvador's family. And his wife, I knew her and I liked her. She had a lover, too. A young Indian man who rode a motorcycle. He was tall for a Guarani—big and strong with long dark hair. She was a beautiful woman, always smiling. The mother of Salvador's children—his twin girls and the little boy, Federico. They spoke Spanish, Italian, and French. They had large gatherings every Sunday at their house. Family and friends of all kinds gathered for *asados* on their porch. The men roasted meats while the women sipped wine spritzers by the pool, watching the children swim and the dogs chasing kids through the vineyard.

My father wanted to know more. I told him about Pinochet. Salvador had lost several friends and family members. University students who were kidnapped, tortured, and killed. Salvador was studying medicine. After one of his friends was found gagged and castrated on the shore near La Serena, he fled to Spain, where he changed his studies to business. He moved to Milan, where he met Octavia, who became his wife. She had fled Chile because of Pinochet, too. They stayed there until they felt that it was safe to go back.

My father asked me if I was in love. I said we had a nice time together. I didn't tell my father that the man asked me to marry him the week before I left. I said to him, "But you're married."

"Details," he replied. I asked him if he would give me two days to think about it. Part of me wanted to stay. I loved being in Chile. I had good friends. I liked the food, I liked his family and his house. I saw myself as a thirty-year-old sitting topless by his pool with his topless ex-wife, and us watching our children play, complaining about the new maid who didn't properly iron the shirts and who was maybe nicking things from Honório and Gerónima.

After the two days, I told him thank you, but no, I have to go to school.

When I got home, my father wanted to know about the sex. He asked if we could smoke cigarettes out by the car. We left the Italian restaurant and I gave him a Camel. We smoked. I was angry and uncomfortable and I told him that no, the man in Chile wasn't circumcised, after my father asked me. He asked if I used birth control. I told him yes.

The man in Chile was me trying to break with my father and me going closer. I didn't see it then. I understood my great rebellion to be something all mine and something new. Something entirely separate from my past. But Salvador was a part of it. He was the next phase of my love affair with my father. After many Sundays with the family, I affectionately called his parents my *abuelos*. I was close to his sisters, his nieces and nephews, his cousins. I became a part of the family. Our sex was a secret. His daughters, Génesis and Anaís, and his little boy, Federico, knew me, they knew I was close to their family, but they didn't know that sometimes during the family lunches on Sundays, when I went into the bathroom downstairs, the one down the hall past the mud entrance, the one near the mops and brooms, the dog bowls and the hanging leashes, the bathroom with the bathtub and shower that his niece and I sometimes bathed in together after we went swimming, washing each other with his wife's French rose soap and his turtle-oil hair conditioner, he would follow me in when I had to pee and he would push me up against the sink and we would watch ourselves in the mirror. He watched me, and I watched myself, too. I looked at my eyes, not his. I watched my eyes open and close. I watched my mouth, not his, open and close and gasp. The girls didn't know that. And they didn't know that their father would lie to them and tell them he was having a meeting with Mr. Ruíz, but he wasn't meeting Mr. Ruíz, he was taking the American girl to dinner, to teach her about fish, to correct her appalling grammar, teach her proper Chilean slang and history—the word for *grill* comes from the torture device—to have her try the braided lamb intestines, and to tell her she drinks too much before taking her to a hotel by the hour. The one not too far from the sea. And the girl, the American girl, would put a towel over the television that you couldn't turn off, with the pornography she didn't want there in the background. Their father would laugh at this silly girl putting a towel over the television. And he laughed even harder when he discovered that she didn't know how to properly use a bidet and that she sprayed herself in the face. And he laughed, too, when the condom got stuck up inside her and he had to carefully fetch it out with his fingers, and she was worried, so worried that she would be pregnant. And he wasn't worried. If she were, she'd stay. She'd sleep in his upstairs bedroom in the bed near the dresser with a pistol hidden in the third drawer down. She would look over the railing on the staircase landing at the large living room below, and the dining room with people coming and going, always people in that happy house, women dancing to the radio, slicing green olives to cook with the ground beef for empanadas, rolling out the dough, listening to Luis Miguel, Violeta Parra, the Beatles, and *La Bohème* and swaying their hips to the Colombian music, and the salsa, the cumbia. The cousins and aunts and nieces cooking inside the large open kitchen. Roasting the tomatoes, peeling the garlic, hand-cutting the pasta that dried on wooden racks overnight. Whipping the cream for the fruit mousse. Slicing the cherimoya, the lucuma, the white strawberries and placing them on large platters. Scoring the whipped potato in a grid with fork tines on top of the meat pie. Stuffing the big avocados, stuffing the crabs inside their own shells. Cleaning the fish for soup. Placing raw clams on plates with ice and lemon slices. Placing the kneaded bread in baskets covered with linen napkins and carrying them out to the tables along the porch where the men stand drinking and talking, turning the beef and the pork and the alpaca and the roasting chickens on the giant grill with their long pokers and tongs. Camila the maid exasperatedly picking up after the wild boys, men coming over to talk business in low whispers. The life-size antique horse in the dining room would listen. Listen to the wife complain to Camila about her husband. Her husband, that impossible man, always doing what he pleased. First his cousin Valentina, and now that American girl.

Salvador and Valentina were thrilled by the fact that she looked just like his mother when she was young and he looked just like her dead father. Octavia referred to her husband and his cousin Valentina as Akhenaton and Nefertiti. They would have married each other, but they wanted babies. And they didn't want babies with tails. I liked that he was in love with a woman because she looked like his mother and he like her father. It all fit neatly. They were secrets, their bond was sex and family.

If I got close to him, I got close to their secret of sex and family. That disturbed me, comforted me.

I asked him about his first time. He didn't tell me about his first time, but he says that he took his cousin Valentina's virginity. He says she came to him one afternoon when no one else was there, took down her hair, and unbuttoned her dress and let it drop to the floor.

One day at his house, I saw Octavia being followed by little Federico, who was just the height of her ass. They didn't see me and she didn't think anyone could see them. He followed his beautiful mother and asked her to please fart on his face. "Please, Mama!" he pleaded, laughing and begging her to fart on his face. And then you could see that she did. And he doubled over with delight. "Again, Mama! Again!"

Twice we went to Argentina for the weekend, to Buenos Aires. Salvador told his wife that he had business there, and we went to the airport separately as he'd instructed me to do, and we did not sit next to each other on the flight. He had told me that he didn't actually have business those weekends, but he did. We drove fast along Avenida 9 de Julio, the widest avenue in the world, slipping across lanes as if we were on ice. We drove north to the Rio de la Plata, the silver river, enormous and slow, so wide it's like the sea and so slow it's like a lake. In the marshy, warm, sticky delta air he asked me to wait for him, for just two minutes, he promised he would be right back. For just two minutes he needed to talk to a guy about a thing. And then we would go to the opera at the Teatro Colón, and after that to supper at midnight, and after that back to his apartment with the spiral staircase. It wasn't for two minutes that he met that guy about a thing. As the hours went by, I walked along the delta and watched the sun go down and the pretty lights decorating the docks and the restaurants over the water blink on, and the lights on the boats, little white twinkling lights everywhere. I walked away from the car, and when I couldn't see the car anymore, just the little lights on the boats, there was a moment when no one in the world knew where I was. I was completely unreachable and unfindable. I liked to feel that way for a few minutes— I loved it. I was completely alone in the world and no one knew who I was and those who knew me had no idea where I was. But I was relieved when Salvador finally returned, and he apologized, and we headed back to the city in time for Act II. On the way to the theater he tells me that his parents saw Maria Callas sing there, and that he saw Pavarotti and Igor Stravinsky perform there. He tells me that the chandelier has a thousand light-bulbs, and the French red velvet curtain weighs seven thousand pounds. He boasts of the Stradivarius instruments in the hall, the French stained glass, the Italian mosaic floor. In the long car ride from the Tigre Delta to the downtown theater, he points out the military barracks, the infamous torture chambers from the Dirty War hidden in plain sight in the city. And he points out the buildings brought over on boats during Buenos Aires's prime—when it was the wealthiest city in the world, he tells me. Entire buildings brought over from France and England, India and Greece. He points out the English bell tower, next to the building with the light pole on the very top. I already know that when the light pole blinks green, it means the Argentinian boxer won the fight, and when the light blinks red, it was the foreigner. He asks me how I know this, and I tell him that I have a friend at school whose brother became my friend, too— Dr. Lionel Corelli—and he told me when I was here on a school trip and he gave me a tour of the city. Salvador does not like this, he doesn't like that I got a tour of the city from another man. But Lionel is just my friend, I assure him. He says that men and women are never just friends and it is impossible that this Dr. Lionel Corelli would take me on a tour of Buenos Aires and not want more from me. He was angry. I told him that Dr. Corelli had a fiancée. Salvador told me that gave him zero assurances that Dr. Corelli wasn't also interested in me, and that South American men never have innocent friendships with women. I replied that North American women *can* have innocent friendships with men. Salvador was now driving very fast through the city. He was angry enough about me knowing about the green and red boxer lights on top of the building that we didn't go to Act II of whatever Wagner opera we were going to see.

But he didn't mind Dr. Corelli being a close friend of mine the next time we snuck away to Buenos Aires, when I woke in the middle of the night in excruciating pain. I called my doctor friend at three in the morning, and he was at the apartment within twenty minutes in his pajamas with his medical bag in hand. He examined me and determined that I had a bladder infection. He went out and returned shortly with medication. He told Salvador, *No sexual activity for three days.* And it meant that we missed the opera again the following night, since I didn't feel up to being out that long. I never went to the horseshoe-shaped Teatro Colón; I never saw its chandelier with a thousand bulbs.

I was better quickly, and Salvador wanted to spend the evening in bed before we ate at midnight at Don Paolo. The following morning we returned to Chile.

A week later, I was on a plane to Brazil looking over the favelas, the endless shantytowns surrounding São Paolo. And then another plane to New York, and then another plane back home. My father and my brother picked me up. It was shocking to be home. I felt a pit in my stomach. I felt terrified that I would die of thirst, starvation. My father and brother and I went to a huge grocery store, and I remember walking down the long aisles of American food feeling like I didn't belong at all. I didn't want to come back home, but I did. I didn't want to be around my father, but I was. I keep returning to the scene of the crime. I can't get away. Even in Chile, I couldn't get away.

What the American girl didn't see at that time was that when she was in Chile, she was doing the same thing she had always done. She had become part of Salvador's family and their sex was secret. The man who was older than her father, the man who could very easily be her father. She didn't mind being a secret. She didn't want to be his wife. She wanted to be a secret. She wanted to be important, but she wanted to be a secret. And then she wanted to slip away just like she slipped in. But she would miss him. She would miss being there. A year later, she went back and they had a nice time again. And she was a secret again. This time he and Octavia would be separated and he would have a new woman living in his house. But it didn't stop them from doing just as they had done before. And the new woman would sense it, she knew the American girl was someone to worry about. Her body broke out in rashes when the American girl arrived. I liked that she got rashes when I showed up; I liked having that power.

He asked me to stay, but I said thank you, no. I wanted to go back to school.

Before I left, I went to Octavia's two-story house with a red-tile roof and rang the bell. Her housekeeper answered and let me in. Octavia didn't ask me why I was there, but offered me coffee. As we sipped our sugary coffee, I told her that I wanted to apologize for having had an affair with her husband while they were still together. She took a sip of her coffee, then got up and asked me to follow her. We went down the hall to a bathroom. She pulled up her white skirt and sat on the toilet. She wasn't wearing any underwear. She peed.

While she pulled off a strip of toilet paper and then wiped herself, she said, "Don't worry, *flaca*, there's no need to apologize."

I returned to Chile another time. I was much older. Salvador's children were grown; his girls were women and Federico was a young man in university. Octavia had moved back to Milan. The family had fractured, scattered. The cousins and nieces and nephews had moved away to Santiago, Madrid, London, Los Angeles, New York. He had lost everything in a few unlucky business deals. He had sold his land; his endless lawn was now a neighborhood. He still had his house, but with nothing in it. Just a table, but not the enormous grand dining table from before. A modest oak table with six yellow wooden chairs. Two armchairs were covered in blankets since the upholstery underneath was worn with holes. The life-size antique horse was gone. The pigeons were taking over outside and the mice inside. Camila had almost nothing to clean, and no children to clean up after, but she had a war to wage on the pests. He wanted her to use poison for the mice, but she refused, she used traps and spent hours stuffing cloth into all the holes she suspected they were using to enter the house. She climbed a ladder and put spikes under the eaves of the house. She made a fake owl and put it on a stake in the yard. Salvador and I drank coffee and looked at his empire in decay.

Gerónima had died, but Honório still lived in the adjacent house. He could still walk and talk and look me up and down and wink just like always. He watched the news and ate his quince jam on bread with a glass of wine before bed. His maid was stealing from him, *la gorda*, but they all steal from him, Camila told me, and now there's almost nothing left to steal. And *la gorda* is sweet to him. She doesn't lose her patience with his constant worry and obsessive complaints.

As a little girl I liked my mother to know that I was someone to worry about. That I could take my father away from her.

And I wanted my father to worry that the man in Chile could take me away from him.

My father was so angry with me after I returned from my first trip to Chile. He accused me of hating men. One night in a French restaurant, he yelled at me. I don't remember what about. He threw his napkin at my face. The waiter asked him to please calm down. But he didn't. Then the manager came over and asked us to leave.

One night, my father asked my brother and me to

watch the movie *Death and the Maiden*. It's the story of a woman who years before had been kidnapped and tortured by a South American regime. Her husband unknowingly brings home his wife's torturer as a guest. The wife holds the guest at gunpoint and does her own trial regarding his crimes against her.

Our father was in the other room while my brother and I watched on the small television. When the movie was over, my father came in. He was in a rage. *Did you like it? Did you like it? Did you? Did you?* Furious voice, furious eyes, clenched jaw, furious body leaning over us where we sat. *Did you like it?* His fury grew. *I bet you liked it*, he yelled. *You did, you did you did. Did you believe her? I bet you believed her.*

My father choked me when I was little, but I don't remember him doing it when I was a teenager. The last time my father choked me I was twenty. It happened in the house near the pond. I was half an hour late to his house for Christmas Eve. He and my brother were there waiting for me in the living room. My father was very angry at me for being late, even though I wasn't even late *to* anything—we were spending the afternoon together and then friends of his were coming over for dinner. It made me very anxious when my brother left to go pick up the goose my father had ordered for Christmas Day and left me alone with him. My father was furious. He had a particular rage for Christmas. He picked up the large Christmas tree and threw it against the wall. Glass ornaments smashed. He threw the coffee table, which had a crèche that had belonged to his mother on it, and everything broke. The table, the wooden angels. I stood there silently watching him break everything that was Christmas in the house. My father came at me and grabbed my neck with both hands. He began to squeeze. He said he wanted to finally do it, he said he was going to kill me. I kicked him. I was wearing heels and I drove one into his sternum and he pulled his hands off to move my leg and when he did, I rolled and then moved as quickly as I could to the door and ran out and ran and ran down the street, until I saw a family walking their dog in the cold. "Merry Christmas!" they said. I asked if I could use their phone. "What's the matter?" they asked me. "I had a fight with my father."

"Go apologize to him," the father said. They let me go to their house and use their kitchen phone. I called my mother and told her what happened and asked her to come pick me up. She said she didn't want to drive that far. I went back to my father's house. He was standing, rocking back and forth, back and forth, on the front lawn. His eyes were other. They were possessed. He was clenching his jaw. "Merry Christmas," he said angrily, and we went inside. He poured me a glass of wine. My brother had returned with the goose and was playing Chinese checkers by himself.

knew a girl in college who was extraordinarily clever. She and I had too much to drink one night and she told me her story and I told her mine. Her older brother had sex with her and had her jack him off in the shower from the time she was around eight or nine and throughout her teenage years. One day their mother walked in and saw them having sex. Lucy was about eleven. The mother walked out of the son's room and never did or said anything about it. These secrets are the most protected things.

The girl had promise. I thought she was going to do so much with her cleverness, wit, and beauty. The other day I heard from a friend that Lucy committed suicide.

In college, Lucy had a boyfriend who was a musician. He wrote a song for her on one of the bridges near our school. He named the song "Lucy's Bridge to Heaven." Lucy and I weren't good friends, but we were competitive classmates. We were the top students in philosophy. I was interested in the idea that language preexists us. I was interested in the idea that morality is only a construct. If there is no intrinsic right and wrong, then what happened to me is something that I can think my way out of.

Lucy and I tried to outdo each other by knowing more obscure writings by Lacan than the other. Lucy liked Derrida more than I did, and I liked Deleuze more than she did. Could *Anti-Oedipus* help me? I wanted desperately to find help inside it. I bought two copies in case that would help me more. I was standing on a bridge over the river when someone told me that Deleuze had just died. It wasn't Lucy's Bridge to Heaven, it was one farther upriver.

I returned home from college for the summer. I lay in my mother's bed for days. I had horrific nightmares. Images of little girls being impaled and dying, then being devoured by ants and maggots. I lay there in the same bed that my father had bought for my mother and himself decades before. The same mattress. My brother was conceived in that bed. I was raped on that mattress. My mother joined me at night. Carefully, frightened by me, she would slip under the covers on the other side, read for a while, then set her alarm, take off her glasses and place them on the bedside table, tell me *Sweet dreams*, and then shut out the light. In the morning she would rise early and attend to the dogs and cats. I cried until my eyes were red and almost swollen shut. I lay in my mother's bed until finally she came in one day and asked me why. I reminded her what my father did to me. I reminded her that he raped me when I was a little girl. *Remember the blood I showed you? Remember when I cut my legs with a kitchen knife? I was only four years old, cutting my legs.* She sat on the edge of the bed. She touched my arm under the covers. She didn't say anything. She didn't say anything then, or that night, or the next day when I got out of that bed. She didn't say anything ever to me about what I told her and what she already knew.

When my father cut my pussy with the knife, he didn't take me to the doctor. He did it just badly enough, but not so badly that I couldn't heal myself.

Another time, I remember the steak knife being held at my throat and then at his own. I told him not to do it. I told him not to hurt himself.

When I was twenty-one years old, I was date-raped. I worked a summer job in a museum and one of the donors asked that I go to his apartment in order to collect a check. He had a loft in the living room. He invited me to go up the ladder to the loft to look at a sculpture, which I did. He followed me, and when he got up, he knocked the ladder off and it crashed to the floor below. He held me down on my back and raped me. Afterward I tried to leave, but he grabbed me and said that I couldn't. I tricked him by telling him I heard something out the window, and while he was distracted by that for a moment, I jumped off the loft and fell onto the floor. I ran out the front door and into the street and got a cab.

In the emergency room, the staff was all very kind. I didn't even need their kindness, but it was nice. They did an examination and a social worker was there. Then I went home and I went to work the next day. My boss asked me how it went, and I told her not very well. She pressed me, since he was an important donor, and so I told her. She was aghast and told me to take the week off. She said the museum would pay for therapy. I said I was fine. I didn't need time off and I didn't need therapy. The truth was that what happened that night didn't really get to me. I also felt partly responsible for it. We can smell these things. I have a weakness that he sensed. He might not have done that to another woman, but he did it to me. Perhaps I smelled the violence in him and acted differently around him, unconsciously, like I did with Carl. And I knew how to leave my body behind and let things happen to it.

I went through two promiscuous phases. One was just before I got married, and one was twelve years later, after my marriage ended. I did it sometimes with the anticipation of pleasure, but it rarely worked out that way. Sometimes it was only about conquest. Sometimes I didn't have any desire or intention to see these men again, to get to know them, to be their girlfriend. I was not looking for love, nor was I offering it. The first phase began with a man while I was in college. I have no idea what his name was. I only have two images of him—one is of him vigorously shaking a martini for himself and the other is of him deeply tongue-kissing my friend Addison. She was one of my closest friends from school. We spent long afternoons reading in cafés, and sometimes long evenings together when her live-in girlfriend was busy with work. One day she asked me about sex with men. She had never had sex with a man, and she wanted to know what it was like and what were all the things that I had done. She wasn't even sure what a penis looked like. I drew her a diagram of a man's genitalia in my notebook. That night we went out to dinner with some other students and ran into one of my favorite professors. Addison, the professor, and I sat at the end of a long table and drank wine. He went to use the restroom and she drunkenly told me she wanted to watch me have sex with the professor. I said I would love to, but I didn't want to because I liked him so much and knew that I would be very weird afterward—perhaps even completely cold—to him if it happened. He came back from the bathroom and we all laughed and drank more, and it would have been seamless for the three of us to leave together. But I stopped it. I liked him too much. But I was drunk and she wanted to watch me have sex with a man. We went to another restaurant, where we kind of knew the owner. Not long after that Addison and I were in his apartment. I watched him deeply kiss her and take off her shirt and her jeans. She wouldn't let him take off her underpants. I remember them—big white underpants. He wanted us to kiss and we did. I looked into Addison's eyes while I got fucked from behind by this unknown man. I watched her eyes get big. Then she and I left and took the subway home and I stood even though the seats were empty. She told me that it was different than she'd expected. I asked her, different how? She couldn't put her finger on it, she said it was just more than she had imagined.

Then there was the Republican who didn't kiss me, but slowly smelled my entire body for an hour before he fucked me. There was the banker who couldn't stop talking about Winston Churchill, and my friend's older brother. The civil rights lawyer who only used colored condoms and who, after I lent him my car, returned it to me with discarded sandwich wrappers on the floor in the backseat. But for the twelve years I was married, I was faithful to my husband.

I loved Isaac. We got married on a boat in our bathing suits. With his father's help, we bought a rambling apartment with three fireplaces near the park. Isaac didn't want children and I did, so we got big dogs. Isaac went to work early in the morning, and before he left, he brought me coffee in bed. He worked a lot. He suggested that I decorate the apartment. I spent my days finding things in antique stores. I spent weeks deciding which stove to get. Which bathtub, which fabric for the guest room curtains. After months of looking, I finally found the cutting sink I wanted for the pantry. I learned to squeeze the juice of a lemon on a wooden cutting board to get out the smell of garlic. And to use baby powder to quiet squeaky wood floors. From Martha Stewart I learned that when you are removing a lipstick stain, first scrape off the excess lipstick from the fabric with a butter knife. I liked being a house-wife. And I didn't like being a housewife. I collected china plates, vintage aprons. Old Baedekers, books of maps, books of myths. I put the books on a shelf in the room with the dark red walls and the pale green chairs.

We had a lot of friends and I was lonely. We had dinner parties where either Isaac cooked or I did. He drank and I didn't. We traveled. We had a lot of insurance. He wanted to take care of me, and he did. Sometimes in the afternoons while he was at work, I looked at pornography. I would look at bondage, at submissive women being beaten, at fathers and daughters. It made my cunt hurt to look and I couldn't help doing it.

Isaac told me that the most magical place he'd ever been was the Isle of Raasay. He told me about the limestone cliffs, the lochs and bogs, the eagles. He took me there and I unpacked my clothes and wanted to stay forever. We spent three days in a hotel in an eighteenth-century stone building, wandering the moors and the beaches. But we barely spoke. The sexual desire wasn't deep and it wasn't wide. In all the years we were together, I never had a dream about him. I never wept on his chest, telling him how terrified I was. I never pulled his chest hair with my teeth and then kissed him, the way I later would with Carl, pulling on his hairs with my hands like an animal, pulling on him, calling to him, saying his name in a soft voice, a baby voice, calling him to do it to me again.

I wanted a safe and calm home. I wanted a sexless home, but I didn't know that then. I wanted him to raise me. And sometimes he did. He taught me about wine and contemporary art. He taught me how to behave at a cocktail party, which I also didn't know, and I never did well. I cut my hair short like he wanted. I stopped wearing lipstick because he didn't like it. And then I wanted him to stop raising me. I wanted my hair long, I wanted to do things besides decorate our apartment and roast lamb for his friends whom he also called mine. I wanted to wear lipstick. After we separated, I felt my back and my arms for the first time in years. I started drinking. I wore earrings.

Sex is the center of things. If you're having it, it's the center. If you're not, it's the center.

Isaac was kind and supportive of me when I told him that my father had molested me. I didn't tell him any more than that. No details, no stories, not for how long or how often. Nothing about my desire and excitement when I thought about what had happened to me. I never said the word *rape* to him. I couldn't say it until very recently. I wouldn't buy grape-seed oil because it had the word *rape* in it. I kept the word out of our home.

Isaac treated me delicately. He said that whenever he thought about what had happened to me, he didn't want to touch me or upset me. It was as if he were afraid of me. I think he had affairs. He must have. There were years when we almost never had sex. Once, when we were walking in the park, he told me that if I ever were to sleep with someone else, he asked that it not be one of his friends, that I use protection, and that I never tell him about it, ever. This made me think that he was doing that. But I didn't have sex with anyone else. For years I shut off all sexual desire. This was about halfway through my marriage, after the time of my rare afternoons with pornography and my years of obsessive masturbation. I didn't have sex and I didn't think about it. I convinced myself that I was better off without it. That I could only be pure and good without it. Sex was too much pain, too much darkness.

My mother was so distraught by the separation and divorce between Isaac and me that she threatened suicide. I don't know why it got to her like it did. Maybe she, too, needed the safe, calm home that she thought I had with him. I don't know.

Isaac and I had dinner with my father about four times a year. Those were the years when I wore baggy clothes and no makeup around my father; I didn't put effort into my hair, I wore flat shoes. I tried to be as undesirable as possible. I wanted to get all the sex out of us. Each time we saw him—Isaac pointed out to me afterward on our way home—my father mentioned child rape or pedophilia. No matter what the conversation was about, my father found a way to bring up child rape. As a joke, or an accusation of someone, just bringing it up. I hadn't noticed this until it was pointed out to me. I remember one time walking on our way to a Greek restaurant. As we passed a big church, my father said to us, "And this is where they rape children."

fter my divorce, I met Carl. I don't know what made Carl guess that my father had molested me. I had never said a word about my father or my childhood to him. It was the first time I ever saw Carl drunk. He wanted to know what my father did to me. He was angry. I said that I would tell him the following day, that I didn't want to have a conversation like that when it was late, when he was drunk and I was tired. But he insisted and I gave in. We went to a bar so I could get drunk, too. I told him that my father had raped me. I didn't tell him any more than that. We went back to his place and he wanted to fuck me. He wasn't fucking me, though, he was fucking me as a little girl.

He poured champagne on my tits and told me I was forbidden to ever cry about my father again—as I had just done—because from now on he wanted to be the only man to make me cry.

I don't like pain, but I desire pain from Carl. I like it when he pushes on my wounds. It makes them feel better. I like it when Carl hits me. I like it when he bites me. I like it when he holds me down and I squirm, which makes him fuck me harder. And if I cry, harder still. I like it when I have marks from him. Marks I carry around with me, like badges on my body. I want him to abuse me. I like it when I can't tell the difference between sexual pleasure and sexual pain—when they are the same. The fact that my father raped me makes him want me more. When I told him about my father tying me up and putting me in the closet, Carl said that was his now, he owned all of it. Carl tied me up and put me in the closet. He let me out and face-fucked me. How could I not love the man who set me free?

We are most who we are in bed, Carl said.

Out in the world, Carl is charming, soft-spoken. Sometimes Carl is even shy. When we first met, my friends thought Carl was calm and gentle. The man with the holes in the elbows of his gray cardigans. At the beginning, that's what I thought, too. I thought he was *too* gentle. For months after we met, even after we became friends, I thought sex with him would be boring.

But the first time that I saw his penis—full of blood after we had taken a nap together on a twin bed in his mother's summer cottage—I knew he was the one. I fell in love with his cock. It was the most beautiful thing I'd ever seen. Nothing like that had ever happened to me before.

That afternoon when I first saw his penis in the daylight, Carl made me a whitefish sandwich, which I ate on the porch while he read Kleist to me. Carl sipped bourbon and took two cigarette breaks. I couldn't stop thinking about his cock. The size, the shape, the pink of the head. Just like my father's.

I pull down art books from his bookcases. I look at the carnivals in Ensor, the contorted pink and yellow faces, his fat pope, the death mask. I look at a breastfeeding Byzantine virgin with her long, stretched-out nipple between her baby's lips. I look at Velázquez's old woman with the spoon, at the egg in the boiling water. I look at the overwhelmingly gorgeous Saint John the Baptists— Andrea del Sarto's and Caravaggio's. Fede Galizia's cherries, her pears, figs, rabbit, sliced-open melon. Piet Mondrian's sharp and pure country drawings. Morandi's bottles and vases and jars.

Carl is a tall man like Morandi. He has stinky feet

from wearing Italian loafers with no socks in the summer. He eats grapes with a fork. Sometimes he runs a fork over my back, writing words that I can't recognize. There are times when I'm not afraid of him at all. Times when all I want is to bring him back to life when he is joyless. Sometimes the only thing that makes him feel good about himself is to overpower me.

I used to go inside my father. I wanted to be the man who hurts girls. Now I go inside Carl. I fantasize about Carl finding women in the streets, fucking them without knowing their names, smashing his hand over their eyes while he fucks them, licking one's pussy while he fucks another, while I'm tied up in the corner watching it all. I go inside Carl when I'm bound and gagged and my face is slapped and I'm told to be a good girl. I want to be a good girl. And I'm the man with the whip.

He likes to choke me with my embroidered pillowcases. So hard sometimes I see stars. He tells me that the more pain I feel, the more I know he loves me.

Carl likes it when he comes home and I'm waiting for him, on my knees with my mouth open. He likes that I'm desperately excited being tied naked to a tree, waiting for him, then untied and bent over to be fucked by him. He likes watching me truss the chicken after I stuff the cavity with shallots and lemon for him. He likes how I walk. He likes my awkwardness. He says he sees something very innocent in me, even now.

I read that you can tell a history of violence in how people walk. I think I walk with assurance, but maybe Carl sees something else. Maybe I can never hide it. It's in how my body moves. My gestures, how I talk.

When Carl once asked me how many men I'd been with, I lied and said five. The truth is I'm not quite sure. But it was more than five. One man had long hair and cowboy boots. I was at a bar waiting for friends; I was in college at the time. He asked me what I wanted to do with my life. I told him that I was going to have my stories in *The New Yorker*. He told me I looked like a girl who had been molested by her father. I thought that he must have had some divine power to know that. I'm sure it was just a sick line, but no one in my life would talk about it, and here was a man who knew it without me saying it and he wanted me to talk about it. He said he could see it in my eyes. I was amazed that he could see that in my eyes. He was staying at a hotel. He told me I had three choices: he could make sweet love to me, fuck my brains out, or we could just talk for a while. I chose just talking for a while, but I was already in his hotel room at that point and I didn't know that meant I had also said yes to the other two options. He left huge hickeys on my neck. I haven't told Carl about that man.

I haven't told Carl about the economist who liked my pubic hair full, a full bush to rub his face in. And the carpenter who asked me to sit on his counter naked in blue high heels while he sipped vodka and cooked me dinner. I haven't told Carl about having sex with my childhood crush, Katherine Huntington's nephew—when we were teenagers—on a sofa in his family's living room, under a duvet, only feet away from his cousins playing cards. We thought we were so sneaky and clever and that no one could tell, since we moved so very slowly and so quietly with our hands clamped over each other's sweaty mouths. But when we emerged with our hair staticky from being under the blanket, the room had emptied.

I haven't told Carl about how long it went on with my father. I haven't told Carl about how I smell strawberries when I think about fucking my father, or how I see black, shiny ants devouring my girl corpse when I remember fucking my father. I haven't told Carl that remembering these things, and remembering my father's open mouth when he was about to come, makes me smell and taste sweet strawberry shortcake.

I pick up *Woodcutters* from Carl's bedside table, and he is using a photo of me as a young girl for his bookmark. I ask him where he found that photograph. He said he went through my things while I was out and found it in my box of stationery and paper clips. He says he likes to look at that little girl and think about defiling her.

He tells me that he imagines me as a little girl when he has sex with me. He told me that he masturbates to that photo of me standing on the beach on the island. In the photograph, I am about nine years old, wearing my black-and-white bathing suit. Your thighs, he says, your little-girl thighs.

I feel myself hot and light. I feel frozen. I have no mind, no body, and I am all mind and all body. I feel him thrusting and moaning while he fucks my little face. He puts his hand around my throat. He squeezes. I go up to the top of the sky and I sit on a cloud. He's choking me. I'm a six-year-old in my frilly white Easter dress. My vision is getting blurry. I'm flying up over the sea and into the stars.

Doesn't it taste good? It's all mine when it's in my

mouth. I remember the taste of the milk chocolate Easter eggs and the yeasty taste of his genitals. I think about Jesus' body in the tomb with the heavy gray stone. Soon the stone will be moved by angels, and very soon he will be released and set free to live forever. I look down at the green field from the clouds while I'm tied to this chair.